THE ZONES OF REGULATION®

A CURRICULUM DESIGNED TO FOSTER SELF-REGULATION AND EMOTIONAL CONTROL

Written and Created by

Leah M. Kuypers, MA Ed. OTR/L

Social Thinking.com

The Zones of Regulation®
A Curriculum Designed to Foster Self-Regulation and Emotional Control

Written and created by Leah M. Kuypers, MA Ed. OTR/L
www.zonesofregulation.com

Edited by Sandra Horwich, Sandra Horwich and Associates, Inc., and
Ann L. Pendley, PhD, CCC-SLP

Library of Congress Control Number: 2011930494

ISBN: 978-0-9825231-6-2
052014

Think Social Publishing, Inc.
Social Thinking Publishing
3031 Tisch Way, Suite 800
San Jose, CA 95128
Tel: (877) 464-9278
Fax: (408) 557-8594

This book was printed and bound in Tennessee by Mighty Color.
Books may be ordered online at www.socialthinking.com.

To all the students I have worked with,
who inspire me,
motivate me,
and help me to grow.

Table of Contents

Foreword
for The Zones of Regulation®

By Michelle Garcia Winner

Teachers, parents, occupational therapists, counselors, speech language pathologists, and others are interested in learning about our students' different sensory, social learning, executive functioning, and emotional regulation needs, but they struggle to find ways to incorporate these different areas of need into a more integrated teaching approach. "Behaving oneself" requires our students to carry out a desirable action while simultaneously thinking, monitoring, and controlling their behavior on many fronts.

Over the past 10–15 years, it has become generally recognized that our students who have self-regulation challenges—whether we refer to these students as having an Autism Spectrum Disorder, ADHD, Non-Verbal Learning Disability, behavioral challenges, etc.—appear to benefit both from some common treatment approaches and from increasing their understanding of their learning needs. This has led to the creation of specific programs to help explain their learning differences, such as the SCERTS® Model (Prizant, et al. 2006), Ziggurat Model (Aspy & Grossman 2007), The Comprehensive Autism Planning System (CAPS) (Henry & Myles 2007), as well as the ILAUGH Model (Winner, 2000). These programs highlight areas that our students need to learn more about, including the following:

- Sensory integration and regulation, helping them learn to manage sensory input from the environment so they can process and respond in ways in which they are expected to function.

- Emotional self-understanding and emotional self-regulation. Emotions can confuse or overwhelm our students. It's key to help them learn to understand the connection between their sensory systems, their emotions, and their ability to relate to the world in ways that make others feel comfortable relating to them.

- Executive functioning and cognitive control of behaviors. These brain-based skills, such as impulse control, sustaining attention, planning, problem solving, and self-talk, serve as the foundation to manage one's functioning in life and overcome the hurdles that stand in the way in reaching a goal.

- Visual scaffolds and visual teachings. Our students, even the "highest functioning" ones, usually benefit from structured visual information. Not only does visual structure cater to the visual learning style of many of our students, but it also encourages us as caregivers to take abstract lessons and present them in more concrete, visually based teachings. Even students who are not visual learners can benefit from highly visual, well-organized material, just as those of us who are not auditory learners can benefit from clear auditory instruction.

- Social Thinking® and related Social Thinking vocabulary. The teachings of Social Thinking provide explicit language-based concepts from which people can develop a better understanding of social perspective taking and interpretation of social emotional responses.

- Development of self-awareness. This is a critical factor in any program encouraging internal regulation of any concept or related skill.

In addition, many other resources, such as Carol Gray's Social Stories® (*The New Social Story Book*, 10th Anniversary Edition, 2010) and *Comic Strip Conversations* (1994), and Dunn Buron's and Curtis's *The Incredible 5-Point Scale* (2004) help to foster the development of some of the different areas described above for students.

In 2009, I first heard Leah Kuypers speak on The Zones of Regulation®, a concept she developed based on her graduate studies and teaching experience and then documented when a graduate student in Education. While writing The Zones of Regulation curriculum she also received guidance from Kari Dunn Buron, one of the two creators of *The Incredible 5-Point Scale*. The Zones, as the concept is referred to in this book, integrates all of the above-mentioned approaches and teaching tools to help students better understand their needs regulation. The goal of The Zones is to help students develop social, emotional, and sensory regulation.

The Zones provides teachers and parents with very clear instructions to guide their students through a set of sequenced lessons, encouraging students to learn about their own regulation system and how they can adjust it. The Zones uses four colors to help students visually and verbally self-identify how they are functioning in the moment given their emotions and states of alertness. Lessons are designed to help students understand their different internal emotions, sensory needs, and thinking patterns that result in each student shifting from one zone to another. Students explore a variety of tools (sensory supports, calming techniques, and thinking strategies) that they can use to regulate what zone they are in and are taught when, why, and how to use their tools.

The Zones of Regulation also incorporates core teachings from Social Thinking to help students learn more about perspective taking to better understand how being in the different zones impacts others' thoughts and feelings around them. In addition, The Zones curriculum helps students gain an increased vocabulary of emotional terms, skills in reading facial expressions, insight on events that trigger their behavior, problem solving skills, and much more.

As I heard Leah discuss The Zones of Regulation, I was impressed by how she interlaced selected lessons from Social Thinking, such as Social Behavior Mapping, with her knowledge of sensory regulation, and with The Incredible 5-Point Scale into a very practical tool to help students develop improved social emotional behavioral awareness and related responses.

When Leah agreed to work with me to publish this book, we closely collaborated to refine her lessons to aid non-specialized adult caregivers (e.g., teachers and parents), who may have relatively little background knowledge related to those with social learning challenges. By using this book, such non-specialists will be able to help students with these challenges to use The Zones techniques across the home, community, and school environments.

At the same time, specialists who have more basic teaching knowledge will appreciate the melding of different areas of learning needs into one tool they can incorporate into their work with school-age students. Educators and parents as well as specialists can simplify these lessons as needed for students with more involved learning challenges or modify them to be more appropriate for those who are more sophisticated learners.

I am thrilled to finally see this book in print and hope these teachings will help all of our students better evaluate their current social emotional zones and make better choices to regulate their thoughts, actions, and sensory needs in a manner that helps them feel proud of themselves for working to be more responsible members of their community.

Michelle Garcia Winner

Chapter 1

Get Ready...

Understanding the Curriculum

"My reputation in elementary school was shaded with impulsive, erratic behavior, temper tantrums, and the worst report card possible, but I also was known for unique and creative abilities."

—Temple Grandin in *Emergence: Labeled Autistic*

Temple Grandin's description of elementary school rings true for many; too often students are struggling to keep it together...while falling apart. Frequently students' shortfalls and disruptive behaviors overshadow their strengths and abilities. Rather than helping to fix the behaviors, people seem to keep pointing them out. Ross Greene, an expert psychologist on treating explosive children and creator of Collaborative Problem Solving, says, "Children do well if they can" (*The Explosive Child,* 2005, p. 16). This is a good mantra for all educators and caregivers. No student wants the reputation as the "bad kid," but they may not have it in their skill set to act differently—unless they have been taught the correct tools to do so and given numerous chances to practice. Students can find success in school, the home, and the community, and much of that success depends on the ability to control unexpected responses and other maladaptive behaviors. *The Zones of Regulation®* was developed to help students reach that goal.

The Zones of Regulation is a curriculum geared toward helping students like Temple Grandin gain skills in consciously regulating their actions, which in turn leads to increased control and problem solving abilities. Using a cognitive behavior approach, the curriculum's learning activities are designed to help students recognize when they are in different states called "zones," with each of the four zones represented by a different color. In the activities, students also learn how to use strategies or tools to stay in a zone or move from one to another. Students explore calming techniques, cognitive strategies, and sensory supports so they will have a toolbox of methods to use to move between zones. To deepen students' understanding of how to self-regulate, the lessons set out to teach students these skills: how to read others' facial expressions and recognize a broader range of emotions, perspective about how others see and react to their behavior, insight into events that trigger their less regulated states, and when and how to use tools and problem solving skills.

The curriculum's learning activities are presented in 18 lessons. To reinforce the concepts being taught, each lesson includes probing questions to discuss and instructions for one or more learning activities. Many lessons offer extension activities and ways to adapt the activity for individual student needs. The curriculum also includes worksheets, other handouts, and visuals to display and share. These can be photocopied from this book or printed from the accompanying CD.

Who can teach The Zones of Regulation?

The curriculum is designed to be taught by anyone who works with students who struggle with self-regulation. This can include, but is not limited to, special education and regular education teachers, occupational therapists, speech and language pathologists, psychologists, counselors, behaviorists, social workers, and parents. Throughout the text, the user is referred to as "teacher"; however, this does not mean you need to be a classroom teacher to teach the lessons.

Who can benefit from The Zones?

The Zones curriculum is designed for students who struggle with self-regulation, as described more fully in the next section. Sometimes deficits in regulation could be a manifestation of a neurobiological disorder and/or a social-learning challenge, but not everyone who has difficulty regulating has a diagnosis. Initially the curriculum was developed for students with neurobiological and mental health disorders, such as an autism spectrum disorder (ASD), attention deficit hyperactive disorder (ADHD), Tourette syndrome, oppositional defiant disorder (ODD), conduct disorder, selective mutism, and anxiety disorders. However, it became apparent that the curriculum can reach a much broader population. All people in general can benefit from The Zones of Regulation, not just the students. When one student starts using The Zones, often parents and teachers find it helps the other children and even themselves. Adults who teach The Zones report better insight into their own states and become more aware of the tools they can use to regulate. Everyone experiences difficulties in regulation from time to time, prompting many regular education teachers to adopt it for use with their whole class.

The Zones lessons are designed to be used with students as young as preschool age (around four years old) if cognitively they are at or above average intellect, elementary students, secondary students, and adults. Where relevant, the lessons suggest ways to do the activities with younger students (preschool to early elementary years) and older students (upper elementary or middle school through high school or adulthood). More mature secondary age students and adults may feel that some of the activities are too "childish" for them but can still benefit from the discussions laid out in the lessons. The depth of understanding will vary depending on the students' age and grade level, cognition, and maturity, and teaching expectations need to be tailored for specific students and groups. For example, you would rarely set a goal for a preschool student to independently regulate by using a tool when facing a stressful situation. You will want to customize how concepts are presented depending on the age and grade level of the students; with younger students, you'll need to simplify some of the discussions.

Although the majority of the lessons are targeted toward students with average to above-average intelligence, some accommodations are provided to allow you to adapt activities for more cognitively-involved students or those with less language. Students with lower cognition may not develop as deep an understanding of The Zones, but with consistent exposure, many are able to gain awareness of their zones and follow visual supports to guide them to activities that aid in self-regulation. You may need to further adapt the concepts presented when you teach students with cognitive impairments.

The rest of this chapter explores the components of self-regulation, explains how the curriculum developed, and describes The Zones themselves and related vocabulary. In Chapter 2, you'll learn what you need to do to begin using the lessons with your students. The curriculum's lessons are presented in Chapters 3, 4, and 5. Chapter 6 includes additional background information about the conceptual basis for The Zones. The Appendix includes frequently asked questions, a set of goals that can be used for IEP documents, recommended resources, footnotes, and the bibliography.

What is self-regulation?

Self-regulation can go by many names, such as "self-control," "self-management," "anger control," and "impulse control." These terms all describe people's ability to adjust their level of alertness and how they display their emotions through their behavior to attain goals in socially adaptive ways (Bronson, 2001). In other words, self-regulation is the ability to do what needs to be done to be in the optimal state for the given situation. This includes regulating one's sensory needs, emotions, and impulses to meet the demands of the environment, reach one's goals, and behave in a socially appropriate way. For example, given a stressful or frustrating experience, a person who can self-regulate well is able to remain calm and organized to successfully negotiate the event. If a person who struggles with self-regulation encounters the same frustrating experience, he or she will have difficulty coping and display maladaptive behaviors. To successfully self-regulate, three critical neurological components need be integrated: sensory processing, executive functioning, and emotional regulation.

Sensory processing

The first neurological component, sensory processing, describes how you make sense of the information perceived by your sensory receptors (the nerve endings that respond to stimuli) as well as how you organize and integrate the information so that you can act upon it in a purposeful way. For example, the sound of a fire alarm is first perceived by your ear. That information is then relayed to your brain to be interpreted—in this case, as a fire alarm going off. You then determine if this is a stimulus you need to attend to or filter out. (Most likely, action is needed if a fire alarm goes off, but often you don't act when someone else's car alarm goes off because you are so used to hearing that sound.) If you determine that action is needed, your body is organized so it can purposefully respond, such as to calmly walk out of the building.

Sensory processing also includes modulating the amount of sensory input you receive so that you don't become overwhelmed by too much of a stimulus. For instance, many younger children love all of the spinning rides at a carnival and can ride on them repeatedly without becoming dizzy. Adults tend to avoid rides such as the Tilt-a-Whirl so they don't become sick or nauseated by the spinning; they know they need to modulate that kind of stimulus. Another example of modulating sensory input is that many people often unconsciously shut off their radio if they are driving a car and hit traffic. By reducing one sensation (the sound from the radio), they are better able to focus on the more important visual information that they need to process (the road and traffic) and feel more in control.

Sensory processing disorder, also called sensory integration dysfunction, first described by occupational therapist A. Jean Ayres in the 1970s, refers to a person having difficulties with receiving sensory information, processing it, and/or responding to it. Sensory input includes the following types of information: visual, auditory (hearing), tactile (touch), olfactory (smell), gustatory (taste), vestibular (movement and body's relationship to gravity), and proprioception (body awareness).

Difficulties in regulation can result from people not being able to filter out extraneous stimuli or being overly sensitive to small amounts of a sensation that most others don't find offensive or notice (known as being hyper-responsive). For example, a student in the classroom has the relevant stimuli they need to process (e.g., the teacher talking, notes on the board) but may be overwhelmed by all the background sensory information that they have difficulty filtering out (e.g., the tags on their clothing itching, noise in the hallway, excessive artwork/visuals hung in the classroom, smell coming from the lunchroom), resulting in the student appearing distracted, irritated, and restless. In contrast, some people seek out intense input in one or more of their senses to feel just right. This is known as being hypo-responsive to that input and can be very disruptive to others if the sensory seeking is not done in a purposeful and meaningful way. For example, some students need additional movement and deep pressure to their bodies to feel focused and ready to learn and may find ways to experience the movement and deep pressure that is perceived by others as inappropriate (e.g., rolling around on the carpet during circle time, getting out of their chair frequently, bumping into others, hanging upside down from their chair). Giving such students meaningful opportunities throughout the day to experience additional movement, heavy work, and deep pressure (e.g., running a note to the office, pushing the ball cart out to recess, erasing the board, passing out papers) will help those students get the sensory input they need to organize their nervous system and be attentive. Our ability to self-regulate depends largely upon how well our brain organizes the information our sensory system provides. We want to be able to integrate the information to meet a purpose. For example, as we hear someone talking, we want to be able to respond with appropriate speech or other communication. If we see a ball being thrown toward us, we want to be able to respond with our arms outstretched to catch it. At other times, we will want to ignore sensory information to prevent becoming overwhelmed or distracted. The Zones of Regulation addresses sensory processing by helping students understand what supports they need to feel regulated.

Executive functioning

The next critical neurological component of self-regulation is executive functioning, which is a general term that describes the cognitive processes involved in the conscious control of thoughts and actions. Executive functioning can be compared to a command or control center in our brains that oversees actions and mental operations. Our ability to self-regulate depends on the effectiveness of these functions. Numerous mental operations fall under executive functioning, but some that are influential to the ability to self-regulate are: attention shifting (attending to two or more activities simultaneously, such as taking notes while listening to a lecture), working memory (updating and purging "files" in the brain with new information), internalization of speech (self-talk), flexible thinking (considering multiple options), planning (organizing actions and executing a plan in order to reach desired goals) and inhibition (impulse control). When these cognitive processes function adequately, students are better equipped to complete the problem solving necessary to overcome the hurdles they meet. Various teaching strategies, including The Zones, can be used to help students gain skills in consciously mediating their actions, which in turn leads to increased control and problem solving abilities.

Emotional regulation

The third critical component of self-regulation is the ability to control emotions. Emotional regulation can be defined as processes that are responsible for controlling your emotional reactions in order to meet your goal. This includes monitoring, evaluating, and modifying the intensity and timing of your emotional response. Aristotle put it best, "Anyone can become angry, that is easy...but to be angry with the right person, to the right degree, at the right time, for the right purpose, and in the right way...this is not easy." As described in Russell Barkley's research (an internationally recognized authority on attention deficit hyperactive disorder), emotions are automatically triggered in response to events. However, cognitive elements, such as having objectivity (determining the size of the problem), motivation, and understanding others' perspectives are used in regulating the emotion. Students who struggle with these skills have a more difficult time regulating their emotions. These are skills that The Zones of Regulation curriculum addresses to help students become successful in self-regulation.

All three of these neurological components—sensory processing, executive functioning, and emotional regulation—depend on one another. If one of these components does not function adequately, the person's ability to self-regulate will be diminished—so it is important to look at all three. This is a brief overview of self-regulation processes. If you'd like to learn more, you can refer to the literature review available at www.ZonesOfRegulation.com.

The story behind The Zones

As an occupational therapist and autism spectrum disorder (ASD) resource specialist who worked in public schools for several years, I encountered students with all types of disabilities, including physical, mental health, and cognitive disabilities. Regardless of their type of disability, many demonstrated deficits in self-regulation and exhibited disruptive behaviors, such as getting too silly, becoming distracted, shutting down, exploding, or acting out aggressively. Working as the occupational therapist, I worked with students to address their needs in sensory regulation. However, their emotional regulation and control of impulses continued to be a challenge and stand in the way of their successes. It became apparent that there was a need to examine the larger picture of self-regulation as well as to change the culture in which the behavior was viewed and addressed.

Often it wasn't academics that restricted students from inclusion in a regular education classroom, it was their disruptive behavior. From my direct observations, it appeared that many of the methods being used to curb behavior, such as point sheets, level systems, and time-outs, did not address the core issue—building underlying skills. Trying to modify behaviors based on rewards and punishments was not cutting it. In writing about promising school-based interventions for reducing aggressive behavior,

Riccomini, Zhang, and Katsiyannis (2005) report that exclusions are found to be counterproductive in reducing negative behavior and are connected to increased rates of grade detention, school dropout, academic failure, and delinquency. Unfortunately, these management techniques are too frequently employed within the schools.

A common misperception when dealing with disruptive behavior is that we just have not found a strong enough motivator for students to behave. However, students do not act out because of a lack of motivation for a reward. While working toward a somewhat motivating reward outside of the students' high interests can be helpful, personal experience has shown me that students often act out because they don't know *how* to make better choices. Students need to be taught what they could do differently and be given the opportunities to practice the skills in a safe and supportive environment.

Looking at students through a wider lens, there was a need to help students learn to recognize their emotions while they still have some control as well as gain skills in controlling their impulses. Students needed regulation tools they could easily access to calm themselves independently without disrupting the entire class. They also needed to gain skills in their ability to think about others and figure out what the social expectations are in any given setting. Through my coursework and assignments while completing a Graduate Certificate in Autism Spectrum Disorders, an idea to address self-regulation in a systematic and pragmatic way was born—I named this "The Zones of Regulation®" or "The Zones" for short.

I started teaching students the concept of The Zones of Regulation during my occupational therapy sessions and social groups in schools. Witnessing how the concept benefited my students (and with much persuasion from my colleagues), I decided to develop and organize my concept into a curriculum—to be shared with others and reach a greater number of students. The curriculum was first written as a capstone, to fulfill my Master of Arts in Education degree. Kari Dunn Buron (co-author of *The Incredible 5-Point Scale*), as well as Cassie Erkens and Donna Brittain, sat on my capstone committee and offered guidance and insight in turning The Zones concept into a curriculum. Once the capstone was completed, Kari suggested I make some revisions and look for a publisher. Around the same time, I had accepted to present on The Zones at Michelle Garcia Winner's 2009 Social Thinking Providers Conference. Following the presentation, Michelle offered to publish the curriculum and provided further suggestions to strengthen the curriculum. Over the last few years, I feel very fortunate to have the advice and support of such esteemed authors in helping to shape The Zones into what it has become. To read more about the story behind The Zones, please visit www.ZonesOfRegulation.com.

Works that influenced The Zones of Regulation

The Zones is an extension of widely used and respected curricula currently available to teach self-regulation. The concept of The Zones was influenced by Mary Sue Williams' and Sherry Shellenberger's The Alert Program®, commonly referred to as "How Does Your Engine Run?®" (www.AlertProgram.com). This highly regarded curriculum, which is based on an underlying theory of sensory integration, is often used by occupational therapists to teach self-regulation. It aids children, teachers, parents, and therapists to monitor their states of alertness and teaches strategies to help change or maintain states of alertness. Using a cognitive behavioral model with simple, concrete language, the Alert Program helps teach how different levels of alertness feel as well as what sensory supports are calming and alerting, so that the students can self-regulate. The Zones of Regulation builds on the Alert Program by also teaching students how different emotions and thinking patterns impact their level of alertness. Additionally, The Zones promotes the use of sensory supports as well as thinking strategies and calming/mindfulness tools to help students regulate between states.

The concept of The Zones is also an extension of the tremendous work of Kari Dunn Buron and Mitzi Curtis and their Incredible 5-Point Scale (www.5PointScale.com). The Incredible 5-Point Scale is a visual tool to teach a behavior, as well as social and emotional concepts, by breaking it into five parts to illustrate the degrees of the concept. The structured system of the scale helps students systemize and monitor various behaviors, such as levels of self-control and voice volume. By assigning a number to the various degrees of the concept, it becomes easier for the students and teachers to monitor, communicate, and provide feedback on the targeted concept. Similar to the Incredible 5-Point Scale, The Zones uses four degrees to sort emotions and states of alertness.

The Alert Program and the Incredible 5-Point Scale provided a foundation for the development of The Zones of Regulation curriculum. As The Zones curriculum continued to develop, it became obvious that the work by Michelle Garcia Winner on Social Thinking® would be a powerful complement to the lessons. Her collective works in Social Thinking help students understand how others are affected emotionally by their behaviors and how this would affect their relationships with those around them. Understanding this social emotional process is a critical component in emotional regulation. Winner's Social Thinking concepts are referenced throughout The Zones' curriculum.

What are The Zones of Regulation?

The Zones of Regulation is a conceptual framework used to teach students self-regulation. Creating this type of system to categorize the complex feelings and states students experience improves their ability to recognize and communicate how they are feeling in a safe, non-judgmental way. It also allows students to tap into strategies or tools to help them move between zones. The Zones of Regulation categorizes states of alertness and emotions into four colored zones:

The Blue Zone is used to describe low states of alertness, such as when one feels sad, tired, sick, or bored. This is when one's body and/or brain is moving slowly or sluggishly.

The Green Zone is used to describe a regulated state of alertness. A person may be described as calm, happy, focused, or content when in the Green Zone. This is the zone students generally need to be in for schoolwork and for being social. Being in the Green Zone shows control.

The Yellow Zone is also used to describe a heightened state of alertness; however, a person has some control when in the Yellow Zone. A person may be experiencing stress, frustration, anxiety, excitement, silliness, nervousness, confusion, and many more slightly elevated emotions and states when in the Yellow Zone (such as wiggly, squirmy, or sensory seeking). The Yellow Zone is starting to lose some control.

The Red Zone is used to describe extremely heightened states of alertness or very intense feelings. A person may be experiencing anger, rage, explosive behavior, panic, terror, or elation when in the Red Zone. Being in the Red Zone can best be explained by not being in control of one's body.

The zones can be compared to a stoplight or traffic signs. When given a green light (in the Green Zone), one is "good to go." A yellow light or caution sign means slow down or take warning, which applies to the Yellow Zone. A red light or stop sign means stop; when a person is in the Red Zone, he or she needs to stop and regain control. The Blue Zone can be compared to a blue rest area where you pull over when you're tired and need to recharge.

It is important to note and reiterate to students that everyone experiences all of the zones at one time or another; the Red and Yellow Zones are not the "bad" or "naughty" zones. Lesson 4: The Zones in Me reinforces this idea. *Make sure not to tell a student one zone is good and another is bad.* Rather, you will teach students to figure out what zone is expected in given circumstances. If their zone doesn't match the environmental demands and the zones of others around them, you will be teaching strategies to assist them in moving to the expected zone. The Zones of Regulation is intended to be neutral and not project judgment when helping students recognize their levels of alertness and feelings.

It is easy to point out to students when they are in the Red and Yellow Zones. However, if the different colored zones are used only to indicate to students when they are not doing what is expected, they will surely become averse to practicing it. Be sure you provide positive reinforcement when they are in the Green Zone as well as when they make efforts to *remain* in the Green Zone when encountering situations that lead them to less regulated states. When they are in a zone, a simple acknowledgement or labeling of that zone will be helpful in recognizing when they are there.

Zones Vocabulary

Listed below is additional vocabulary that is used in The Zones.

Toolbox: A collection of calming and alerting strategies a student can pull from depending on the present need.

Tools or strategies: Used interchangeably to refer to a calming or alerting technique that aids the student in regulation.

Trigger: An irritant that causes a student to become less regulated and increases the likelihood of going into the Yellow or Red Zone.

Stop, Opt, and Go: A concept used to aid students in controlling impulses and problem solving better solutions. This phrase is paired with a stoplight to provide additional cues for students.

Expected behaviors[1]: Behaviors that give people around you **good or comfortable thoughts** about you.

Unexpected behaviors[1]: Behaviors that give people **uncomfortable thoughts** about you.

What is the size of the problem? and Is this a Big or Little Problem?[1]: Questions posed to help students measure the size of a problem they are experiencing (Big Problem, Medium Problem, or Little Problem).

Big Problems: Problems that many people share and that have no easy, quick, or pleasant solution.

Medium Problems: Problems some people share that are able to be resolved in an hour to a couple of days.

Little Problems: Problems that only affect one to two people and can be ignored or solved in a matter of minutes.

Inner critic: Used to describe negative, self-defeating thoughts.

Inner coach: Used to describe positive thoughts.

Superflex thinking[2]: A flexible thinking pattern in which a person is able to consider different points of view or ways to do something.

Rock Brain thinking[2]: A rigid thinking pattern in which a person gets stuck on an idea and has difficulty considering other options or ways to do something.

1. Social Thinking vocabulary developed by Michelle Garcia Winner, *Thinking About YOU Thinking About ME* (2007)
2. Social Thinking vocabulary developed by Stephanie Madrigal and Michelle Garcia Winner, *Superflex: A Superhero Social Thinking Curriculum* (2008)

Chapter 2:

Get Set...

How to Use the Curriculum

In this chapter, you'll learn more about how to use The Zones curriculum and what you need to do to prepare to teach the lessons. The chapter discusses ways to group students; how to collaborate with others on students' teams; how students can organize their Zones materials; the length, structure, and sequence of lessons; materials you'll need; and how to link The Zones lessons to academic standards.

Forming groups

When putting together a group with which to teach The Zones, it is beneficial for students to have similar cognitive abilities so instruction can be geared to their levels. Groups of two to four students work best, though in a classroom setting with another facilitator, it is easier to have a larger group of eight to ten students. When grouping students, one also needs to take into consideration the students' abilities to reflect on their own behavior and take on others' perspectives. If a student has poor awareness of others, the student may have increased difficulty regulating his or her own behavior to match the demands of the group; that student might work better individually or in a dyad. In some circumstances, students may need to have individualized instruction as they will move through the curriculum at different speeds given their baseline skills in social cognition and self-regulation. Although the lessons are designed for use in a group format, you can easily adapt many of them to work one-on-one.

In the ideal situation, students who struggle with self-regulation benefit from both individual and group interventions. This allows you to tailor The Zones for the student in an individual setting, while also providing the benefit of working in a larger group to address the contributing social factors. Working in a group requires an increased ability to regulate given the greater social demands of having other students to think of and tolerate. Students who are not yet able to work in a group should first start working one-on-one to address their regulation skills.

Collaborating with students' teams

When all team members (other staff, parents, classroom assistants) are on board and familiar with The Zones concepts and terms, it helps to create a comfortable and supportive environment for students to effectively practice their self-regulation skills. The curriculum provides easy-to-distribute information including a letter explaining The Zones concepts (Reproducible A: Information About The Zones of Regulation) as well as a glossary of related vocabulary (Reproducible B: The Zones of Regulation Glossary). Set aside time to talk with parents and staff (teachers, therapists, counselors, administrators, private clinicians, and aides) who work closely with the student about your goals for the student to improve his or her ability to self-regulate and how they can help. At that time, you can also review Reproducibles A and B so everyone has the same understanding. Explain to parents and staff it will benefit the student if they can reinforce Zones concepts throughout daily life in a variety of settings.

By having those who work closely with the students model the language and highlight the concepts in different environments, the students are able to generalize material, become familiar and comfortable with using the language, and establish a common language to communicate their feelings and needs with those close to them. Given the difficulty in predicting when a student will go into the Red or Yellow Zone, it is optimal for all the people who work closely with the student to be aware of The Zones. This prepares adults to help the student find his or her way back to the expected zone without having to "manage the behavior."

As lessons are completed, send home photocopies of completed student worksheets for students to share with their families. Also provide a copy for other adults who work closely with the student who would benefit from being informed. This keeps communication open among the team members and provides the student with support as he or she learns to self-regulate in a variety of everyday environments. It is also highly recommended that ongoing, open communication is established between home, school, and outside service providers so all can be updated on what the student has learned, discuss the photocopied lessons that were distributed, and tailor support to help the student progress. One way to do this is by establishing an online group that all team members are invited to join, such as through Yahoo! Groups. Before discussing a student with others, however, make sure you have written parental consent to talk with that person. Although collaboration among team members can seem cumbersome, it is critical for student success. Research has shown (Miranda, Presentación & Soriano, 2002 and Sofronoff, 2005) that students with ASD and ADHD make more gains when the caregivers and teachers are provided education and strategies to support the students!

Information About The ZONES of Regulation®

_________________________ will be participating in The Zones of Regulation® curriculum (or "The Zones" for short), which are lessons and activities designed by Leah Kuypers, licensed occupational therapist, to help him/her gain skills in the area of self-regulation. Self-regulation can go by many names, such as self-control, self-management, and impulse control. It is defined as the best state of alertness of both the body and emotions for the specific situation. For example, when a student plays on the playground or in a competitive game, it is beneficial to have a higher state of alertness. However, that same state would not be appropriate in the library. The lessons and learning activities are designed to help the students recognize when they are in the different zones as well as learn how to use strategies to change or stay in the zone they are in. In addition to addressing self-regulation, the students will gain an increased vocabulary of emotional terms, skills in reading other people's facial expressions, perspective about how others see and react to their behavior, insight into events that trigger their behavior, calming and alerting strategies, and problem solving skills.

A critical aspect of this curriculum is that all team members know and understand The Zones language. This creates a comfortable and supportive environment for the student to practice his or her self-regulation skills. It also helps the student learn the skills more quickly and be more likely to apply them in many situations. You can support the student during this process by doing the following:

- Use the language and talk about the concepts of The Zones as they apply to you in a variety of environments. Make comments aloud so the student understands it is natural that we all experience the different zones and use strategies to control (or regulate) ourselves. For example, "This is really frustrating me and making me go into the Yellow Zone. I need to use a tool to calm down. I will take some deep breaths."
- Help the student gain awareness of his or her zones and feelings by pointing out your observations.
- Talk about what zone is "expected" in the situation or how a zone may have been "unexpected."
- Share with the student how his or her behavior is affecting the zone you are in and how you feel.
- Help the student become comfortable using the language to communicate his or her feelings and needs by encouraging the student to share his or her zone with you.
- Show interest in learning about the student's triggers and Zones tools. Ask the student if he or she wants reminders to use these tools and how you should present these reminders.
- Ask the student to frequently share his or her Zones Folder with you and talk about what he or she has learned.
- Make sure you frequently reinforce the student for being in the expected zone rather than only pointing out when his or her zone is unexpected.

It is important to note that everyone experiences all of the zones—the Red and Yellow Zones are not the "bad" or "naughty" zones. All of the zones are expected at one time or another. The Zones of Regulation is intended to be neutral and not communicate judgment.

Sincerely,

_________________________ _________________________

(name) (role on team)

The ZONES of Regulation® Glossary

Self-regulation: The ability to achieve the preferred state of alertness for the given situation. This includes regulating one's body's needs as well as one's emotions.

The Zones: A concept used to help students learn how to self-regulate. The Zones of Regulation creates a system to categorize how the body feels and emotions into four colored zones with which the students can easily identify.

Blue Zone: Used to describe a low state of alertness. The Blue Zone is used to describe when one feels sad, tired, sick, or bored.

Green Zone: Used to describe the ideal state of alertness. A person may be described as calm, happy, focused, or content when he or she is in the Green Zone. The student is in control in the Green Zone.

Yellow Zone: Used to describe a heightened state of alertness. A person may be experiencing stress, frustration, anxiety, excitement, silliness, or fear when in the Yellow Zone. The student maintains some control of himself or herself in the Yellow Zone.

Red Zone: Used to describe an extremely heightened state of alertness. A person may be experiencing anger, rage, explosive behavior, panic, extreme grief, terror, or elation when in the Red Zone and is described as being "out of control."

Toolbox: A collection of calming and alerting strategies a student can pull from depending on the present need.

Tools or strategies: Used interchangeably to refer to a calming or alerting technique that aids the student in self-regulation.

Trigger: An irritant that causes a student to become less regulated and increases the likelihood of going into the Yellow or Red Zone.

Stop, Opt, and Go: A concept used to aid students in controlling impulses and problem solving better solutions. This phrase is paired with a stoplight to provide additional cues for students.

Expected behaviors[1]: Behaviors that give people around you **good or comfortable thoughts** about you.

Unexpected behaviors[1]: Behaviors that give people **uncomfortable thoughts** about you.

What is the size of the problem? and Is this a Big or Little Problem?[1]: Questions posed to help students measure the size of the problem they are experiencing (Big Problem, Medium Problem, or Little Problem).

Big Problems: Problems that many people share and that have no easy, quick, or pleasant solution.

Medium Problems: Problems some people share that are able to be resolved in an hour to a couple of days.

Little Problems: Problems that only affect one to two people and can be ignored or solved in a matter of minutes.

Inner critic: Used to describe negative, self-defeating thoughts.

Inner coach: Used to describe positive thoughts.

Superflex thinking[2]: A flexible thinking pattern in which a person is able to consider different points of view or ways to do something.

Rock Brain thinking[2]: A rigid thinking pattern in which a person gets stuck on an idea and has difficulty considering other options or ways to do something.

---

1 Social Thinking vocabulary developed by Michelle Garcia Winner, *Thinking About YOU Thinking About ME* (2007)

2 Social Thinking vocabulary developed by Stephanie Madrigal and Michelle Garcia Winner, *Superflex: A Superhero Social Thinking Curriculum* (2008)

Organizing materials in Zones Folders

Organizational difficulties can be a weakness for many students who struggle with self-regulation. It is recommended that you create a Zones Folder for each student to store the handouts and worksheets they will complete. (Either a two-pocket folder or three-ring binder will work.) You may opt to have students create their own folders in advance, in which case you could ask them to draw a picture of a place they find calming or of themselves doing their favorite activity on the front cover to personalize the folder. If drawing is difficult for a student, a photograph of the student engaged in his or her favorite activity could also be used. Make sure each student's full name and classroom teacher's name is on the folder so it can be returned if it is lost. Have students keep the Zones Folder in a location that is easily accessible. Posting visual supports of The Zones and concepts on desks, walls, calming areas, etc., may be helpful depending on students' needs. You can reproduce the colored and black-and-white handouts on the CD that came with this book.

Encourage students to share the information inside their Zones Folder with other adults and peers. To prevent more of a chance of the Zones Folder getting lost, it is recommended you copy the information to send home or give to other staff instead of passing around the actual folder. Sharing the information allows students to know they are supported in gaining skills in self-regulation and will help them become more confident in practicing their skills and apply them in different environments.

Structure of group sessions

In general, the lessons are designed to be conducted in 30- to 60-minute sessions, which will vary depending on the size of your group, time spent on discussions, and students' abilities. In the beginning of each lesson, background information is included for the teacher to better understand the concept being taught. All lessons are organized in the same order: lead-in, learning activity, and wrap-up. Posting the schedule on the board for each lesson will help students know what to expect within the lesson and will provide structure to ease anxiety. Posting a schedule will also assist students who benefit from external cues to plan and organize their actions. Some lessons include more than one activity or different ways to adapt it for different populations. Other lessons include additional learning activities, which are extensions to the curriculum to further reinforce concepts. You can refer back to previous lessons or worksheets as students build new skills that expand upon those learned previously. For example, as students are learning when to use their Yellow Zone tools (Lesson 14), remind them of their portrait of Me in the Yellow Zone (Lesson 6).

Each lesson includes probing questions for facilitating discussions so students can deepen their understanding and find meaningful connections between the concepts being taught and their own lives.

Once a lesson has ended, it is intended that those working closely with students continue applying the concepts of The Zones in meaningful ways for the students throughout daily life. This can be done by identifying when you or others are in different zones and the tools *you* are using to self-regulate. In turn, you can ask the students what zone they are in and positively reinforce them when they attempt to use their tools. It is also important to process circumstances or triggers with students that lead to a less regulated state and to incorporate The Zones and its related tools to assist them in regulation.

WEIGH STATION ↗

Using journaling as an adaptation

One significant adaptation that can be applied throughout the curriculum is journaling. As an alternative to discussions, you can have students create journals in which they reflect on the questions posed within the lesson. Journaling can be used to assess the depth of understanding of the concepts being taught as well as to address academic standards in language arts. If you have students journal, be clear about your expectations in regard to punctuation, spelling, grammar, legibility, composition, etc... if you are grading on structure as well as on content. A "cheat sheet" may be used as an adaptation to help with spelling, grammar, punctuation, and so on if writing structure is not a concern.

Linking The Zones to academic standards

The Zones of Regulation curriculum can be used as is or appropriately adapted to address K-12 academic standards. The following are some examples of how you can connect the lessons to these standards.

In mathematics, learning activities include constructing and interpreting line and bar graphs. Using The Zones, students are asked to collect data over time and use these data to draw conclusions, e.g., to identify which calming tool within the curriculum of The Zones they found most effective. Learning activities also ask students to discover patterns in the data, such as determining if certain times of the day or school subjects trigger them to be in an unexpected zone.

In the areas of reading and literature, students will increase their vocabulary, most particularly in the area of emotions as they learn to identify a wider range of feelings. Learning activities that incorporate reading books will challenge students' reading comprehension as students are asked to demonstrate literal comprehension, make predictions from illustrations and text, and relate text to prior knowledge and experiences. Students are asked to respond to books of literature using details from the stories that involve characters who struggle with self-regulation to make personal connections, e.g., asking students what tool they would use if they found themselves in a similar situation as that of a story character. Writing and spelling standards can also be areas of focus during learning activities if so desired by the teacher.

As discussions are an aspect of each learning activity, standards in speaking and listening are integrated. Students are asked to communicate effectively through participating in conversations and formal discussions about The Zones concepts: following two-step directions; attending to and understanding the meanings of messages; communicating needs, feelings, and ideas to peers and adults; and using a voice level appropriate for the language situation.

The Zones of Regulation also emphasizes character development, such as attentiveness, truthfulness, respect for authority, diligence, self-discipline, patience, forgiveness, respect for others, peacemaking, and resourcefulness. In addition, this curriculum focuses on nonviolent conflict resolution. The Zones promotes equality, respect, understanding, effective communication, individual responsibility, thoughtful decision making, positive conflict resolution, useful coping skills, critical thinking, and listening and watching skills. This curriculum can also be used as part of implementing Response to Intervention (RTI)—to reduce student behavioral issues and maximize student success.

Checking for learning

Some suggestions for how you can assess for learning are included within each lesson. In addition, ideas for ways to informally check if students are learning the concepts taught in that chapter's lessons are included at the ends of Chapters 3, 4, and 5. These methods can include listening for their depth of understanding when participating in discussions and activities; insights displayed when completing worksheets; direct observation of skills being applied; and reports from students and others who work closely with them. It's important to do these ongoing checks throughout the lessons in each chapter. This allows you to see which students need additional support and which students have grasped the concept and are ready to move on.

The lesson sequence

The Zones of Regulation lesson plans are presented in the next three chapters:

- Chapter 3 introduces the four zones. Learning activities are designed to teach the students to recognize their zone at any given time, gain insight into how their behavior changes how others think and feel about them, understand how their ability to regulate affects their day as a whole, and identify triggers that lead to the Yellow or Red Zone.
- Chapter 4's activities teach students various tools that are calming and alerting. These tools include sensory supports, calming techniques, and thinking strategies.
- Chapter 5's activities teach students why, when and how to use the tools they explored in Chapter 4 to influence their zones. Students also learn how to integrate the use of these tools into everyday life.

The lessons in Chapter 3 and 5 are intended to be introduced in the order they appear to present manageable bits of information that build on one another and to aid you and the students in organizing the information. Chapter 4's lessons may be taught in any order and can be introduced as soon as students are able to decipher what zone a tool would help them in. (For example, if a tool helped them feel calm, it would be useful in the Yellow or Red Zone, a tool that helped them feel more alert would help them in the Blue Zone, and a tool that helped keep them feeling focused would be used in the Green Zone.) This requires students to be able to understand what each zone represents and how it feels to them (Lesson 4), giving them the ability to gauge if a tool would benefit them. (See Figure 1: Road Map of Zone Lessons to be Taught Over the Course of Time for a visual reference of how to sequence lessons.) Ideally, students would explore and practice tools from Chapter 4 on a regular basis at the same time as lessons from Chapter 3 are still being taught. You can do this by setting aside five minutes at the beginning of a group session to practice and reflect on a tool before you introduce the main lesson.

Once students have a handful of tools they feel would help them move between zones, you can teach the lessons in Chapter 5 to assist them to organize tools and become more effective in using them to regulate. The last lesson of the curriculum, Lesson 18: Celebrating My Use of Tools, is a progressive lesson that can be started after Lesson 13 to reinforce students for using their tools. The Zones' License, which is part of Lesson 18, can be handed out after a predetermined amount of Tool Awards! (see Lesson 18) are received or at the culmination of The Zones lessons.

Depending on the students' abilities and grade levels, some of the lessons' learning activities may be more applicable and age appropriate than others; however, all the lessons include relevant discussion questions that can be used to help students deepen their understanding of concepts.

You will find that many of the lesson's activities are most beneficial if they are presented more than once or on a regular basis so students can

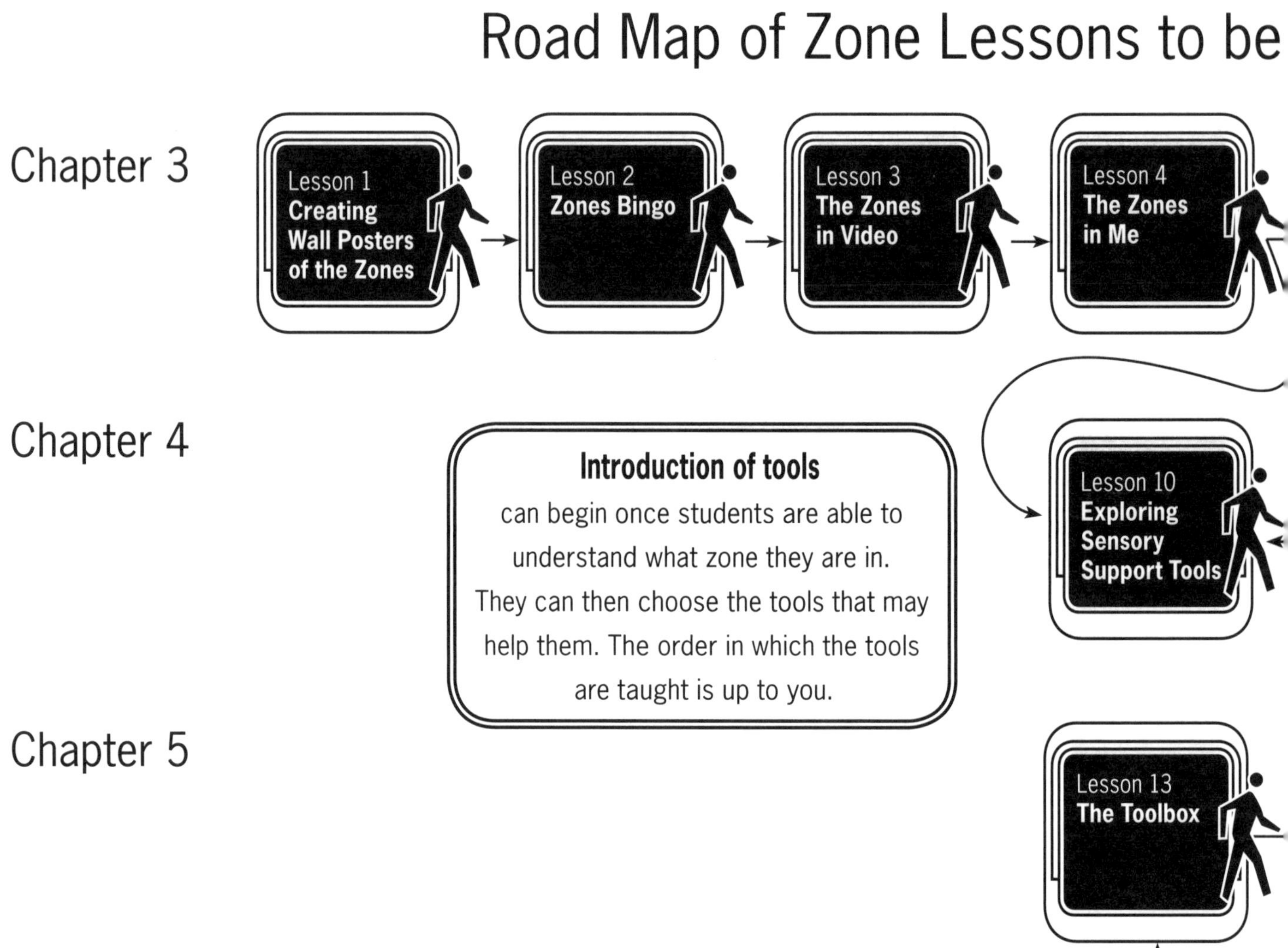

Figure 1: Road Map of Zone Lessons To Be Taught Over the Course of Time

fully comprehend the concept being taught and put the skill into everyday practice. This is often the case in the lessons after Lesson 4.

Learning how to self-regulate is a skill that doesn't develop overnight. It takes time, patience, understanding, and support. How long it takes students to learn independent regulation will vary greatly, with some able to move through the lessons in weeks and generalize the concepts into daily life with little effort. With other students, it is a much longer journey. It is okay to take a break from the curriculum for awhile if a student isn't progressing or able to grasp the concept introduced. With time comes maturity and cognitive growth, possibly putting them in a better place after a hiatus of a couple of months. During a break, you can continue to reinforce and help them apply what they have already learned.

Gathering materials

A supplemental CD inside this book's back cover includes a printable version

Taught Over the Course of Time

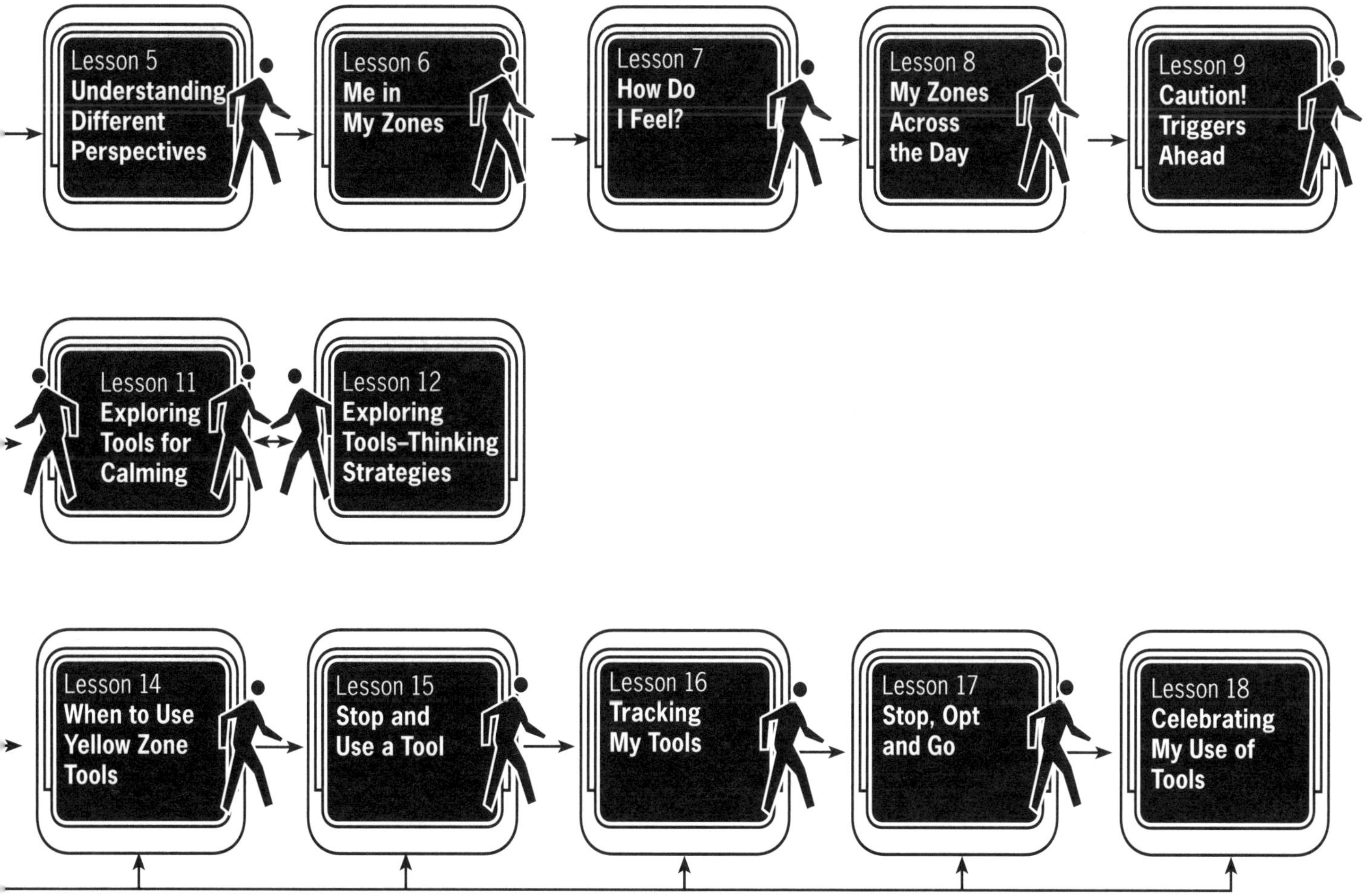

Start rewarding for use of tools (see Lesson 18) as soon as students start using them.

of all the reproducible handouts and worksheets referred to throughout the curriculum. The reproducibles in the book are all in color, while the ones on the CD include a color version and a black-and-white version for printing. Although the majority of preparations can be done before each lesson, there are some recommended materials that may take longer to obtain. These include the following:

- Colored construction paper in four zone colors plus black
- Colored pencils, markers, or crayons in zone colors
- A permanent black marker (fine tip works best)
- A pocket folder or three-ring binder for each student
- For younger students: A copy of the book *On Monday When It Rained,* by Cherryl Kachenmeister (1989) or *The Way I Feel,* written and illustrated by Janan Cain (2000) (for Lesson 1)
- Magazines that can be cut from (for Lesson 2)
- For older students: A copy of the movie *The Outsiders* (Zoetrope Studios, 1983) (for Lesson 3)
- For younger students: A copy of *Charlie Brown* films, TV specials by Charles Schultz, or *Finding Nemo* by Disney (2003) (for Lesson 3)
- A Polaroid® or digital camera and related equipment for printing pictures (computer, printer, and paper) (for Lessons 6 and 18)
- *Miss Nelson Is Missing* by Harry Allard and James Marshall, (1977) (for Lesson 6)
- For younger students: *Do I Feel? An Interactive Reading Book of Emotions* by Joan Green (2004) (for Lesson 7)
- For older students: *I Have Feelings, Too! An Interactive Reading Book of Emotions for Teens, Adults and Seniors*[2] by Joan Green (2004) (for Lesson 7). **Note to teacher:** The graphics in this book may be seen by some adolescents as childish.
- Sensory tools to explore, which could include any of the following: a fidget ball or Silly Putty®/theraputty; rice bin; weighted blanket, vest, or lap pad; sitting on a Move-n-sit or Disc-o-sit cushion (both examples of inflatable cushions that provide a student seated on it with a subtle movement experience); noise-canceling headphones; scooter boards; a jump rope or trampoline; bike or scooter; bean bag or oversized pillow; therapy ball (for Lesson 10)
- A sponge or foam block (often mattress stores or factories will give out foam scraps) (for Lesson 12)
- Duct tape (for Lesson 12)

Supplements to the curriculum

To supplement the curriculum, recommended resources are included in the Appendix. This contains information on strategies, approaches, and techniques, including the original works published by the credited authors that are cited within The Zones. In addition, supplemental information, books, and tools from other resources that can be used to help reinforce learning are listed in the Recommended Resources section. Given there is a need for students to understand perspective taking in order to self-regulate, lesson plans on Social Thinking® concepts by Michelle Garcia Winner have been adapted (with permission) for use with The Zones of Regulation curriculum and are made available in this book. This is for the ease of the reader, so that Winner's concepts can be explored with students in order to complement The Zones' lessons on self-regulation. An excellent complementary curriculum to The Zones are Winner's books, *Thinking About YOU Thinking About ME*, 2nd edition (2007) and the companion curriculum, *Think Social!* (2005).

Chapter 3

GO!!!

Introducing Students to The Zones

In the lessons in this chapter, students learn that they have zones or different levels of alertness and emotional states of being. The activities in these lessons are designed to help students expand their emotional vocabulary, recognize emotions in themselves and others, understand how their states affect those around them, and increase their awareness of triggers that lead to less regulated states. Students become aware that their emotions and sensory and physiological needs, as well as their environments, can influence which zone they are experiencing. They learn that all of the zones are expected at one time or another. By participating in a variety of activities, students see that they know The Zones vocabulary and can let others know when they use it. The focus is on self-awareness at this point in the curriculum. At the end of the chapter, "Ways to check for learning" suggests methods you can use to determine if students are grasping the concepts: Check-In, Zones Flip Book, and Wall Posters.

Goals for this chapter

By the end of the chapter, students will be learning to:

- Develop the ability to identify a range of emotions and how they relate to a student's specific zone (Lessons 1, 2, 3, and 7)
- Read their own body's cues regarding what zone they are experiencing (Lessons 3 and 6)
- Develop insights on triggers and circumstances that influence their zones (Lessons 4, 8, and 9)
- Relate how their zone and behaviors have changed others' perspectives (Lessons 3, 4, 5 and 8)

In the lessons in this chapter, students consider the following essential questions:

- What are the zones?
- How will they help you identify what emotion or state of alertness you are feeling?
- How do different emotions play different roles in different zones?
- How does the way you act in the different zones affect the way other people perceive you?
- How can you benefit from understanding what makes you change zones?

Note to Teacher

At this point it is expected that you have already worked to set up students' Zones Folders as described in Chapter 2.

Lesson Plans and Learning Activities

Lesson 1:
Creating Wall Posters of The Zones

Goals for this activity

- Students become familiar with the concept of The Zones
- Students increase emotions vocabulary
- Students increase recognition of facial expressions

Materials

- ☐ Two 12" x 18" pieces of construction paper in each of these colors:, green, yellow, red, and one piece in blue (known as "zone colors")
- ☐ A piece of black construction paper
- ☐ Markers in zone colors
- ☐ Glue
- ☐ Scissors
- ☐ One copy of the Zones Emotions (see Reproducible C)
- ☐ Software such as Boardmaker™ (www.mayer-johnson.com) can be used as an alternative to create "feeling" pictures
- ☐ One copy of Zone Labels (see Reproducible D)
- ☐ One copy of The Zones of Regulation visual (see Reproducible E) per student
- ☐ **For older students:** Container in which to put the cut-out pictures, such as a hat, bucket, or jar
- ☐ **For younger students:** *On Monday When It Rained,* by Cherryl Kachenmeister or *The Way I Feel*, written and illustrated by Janan Cain

Overview

This activity introduces students to the four zones used to categorize the different emotions and states of alertness people experience while creating visuals to display in the classroom (see Figure 2). Using images of various feelings that are drawn from a container or descriptions of feelings read from a book, students learn to identify the four zones that are the foundation of the curriculum. Students also work on increasing their vocabulary of emotions and recognition of facial expressions.

Preparation of the wall posters of The Zones (will be filled in later with students):

- Print one copy of the Zones Emotions from this book or the CD (Reproducible C). **For older students** – Cut out and place in the container all of the pictures of emotions and states of alertness. **For younger students** – Cut out and set aside the emotions that correspond with the feelings in the book.
- Cut out traffic sign shapes from the construction paper. You will need to tape together the two pieces of construction paper of each color except blue to make the visuals big enough (red for an octagon/stop sign—14"x 14" square with the four corners cut off to make an octagon, yellow for a diamond/caution sign—14" x 14" square turned to form a diamond, green for a circle/go light—14" circumference, and blue for a rectangle/ rest area sign—you can use the full sheet of blue construction paper).
- Cut out four traffic sign posts from black construction paper (1" x 12" strips). Affix the posts to the four signs (see Figure 2). **Note to teacher**: For a simpler visual display, you can tape together the four shapes made of construction paper in the following order left to right: blue, green, yellow, red.
- Color in the Zone Labels (if you did not print them in color) and glue them in the center of each corresponding shape of colored construction paper. Hang The Zones of Regulation label above where you will post the Zones wall posters.
- Hang the Zones wall posters in the classroom where students can easily read them.
- Write this schedule on the classroom board:
  1. Lead-in
  2. Create wall posters of zones
  3. Wrap-up

Lead-in for all ages

1. Get students interested by asking if they believe they can categorize all the ways we feel and act into four groups or zones. Introduce the concept of the zones with the wall posters for a visual:
   - There are four zones that we will use to describe how your brain and body feel.
   - When you're in the Blue Zone, your body is running slow, such as when you are tired, sick, sad, or bored.
   - The Green Zone, like a green light, is when you are "good to go." If you are in the Green Zone, you may feel happy, calm, and focused.
   - When entering the Yellow Zone, proceed with caution and slow down! The Yellow Zone describes when you start to lose control, such as when you are frustrated, overwhelmed, silly, wiggly, excited, worried, anxious, or surprised. It is a good idea to use caution when you are in the Yellow Zone.
   - The Red Zone is reserved for extreme emotions such as terror, uncontrolled anger, aggression, and elation. When you are in the Red Zone, you are out of control, have trouble making good decisions, and must STOP.

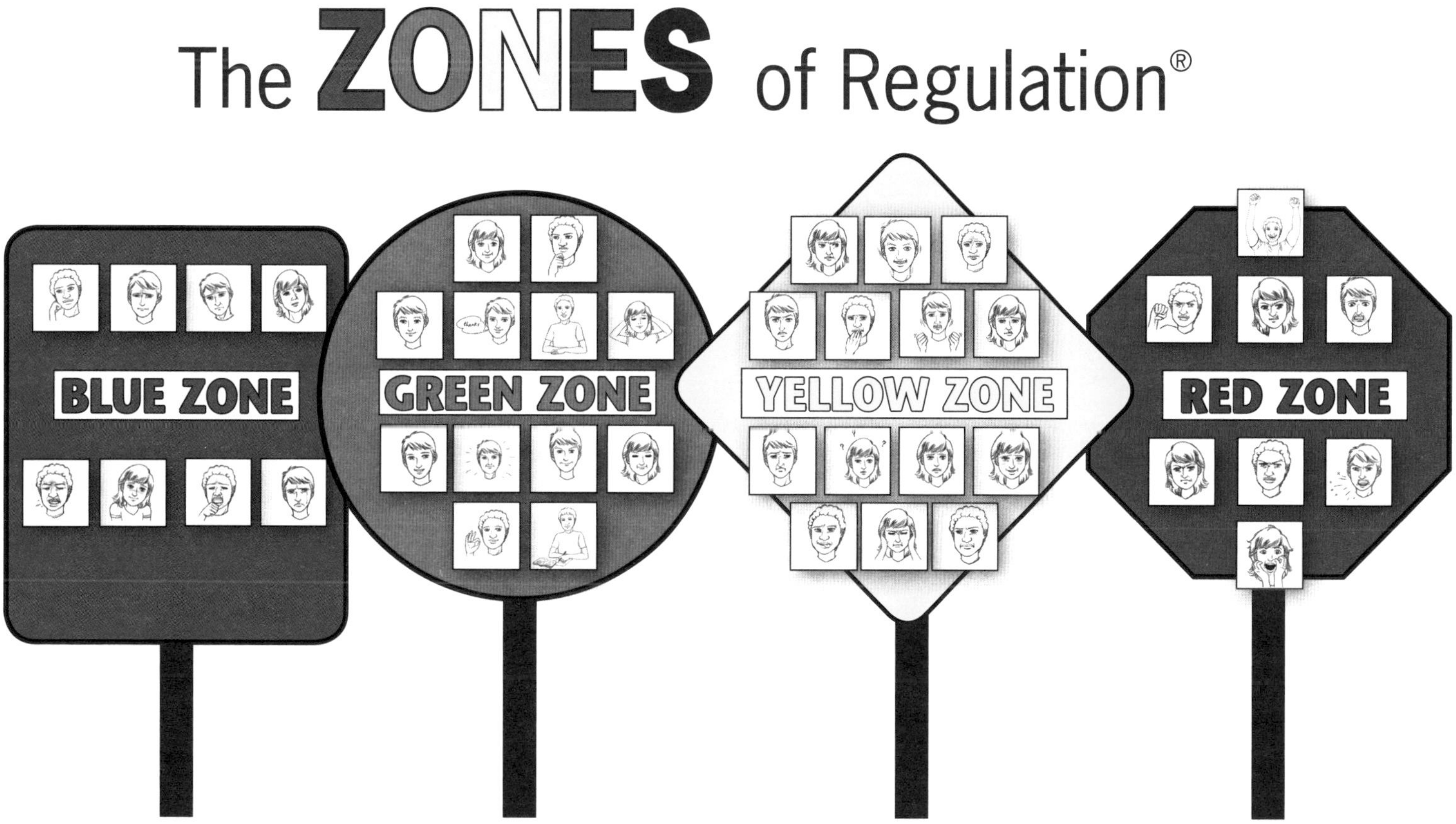

Figure 2: Wall Posters of the Zones

2. Review with students the goals of the activity. Explain that they will be participating in an activity to categorize emotions and different ways they feel into the four zones.

Activities for different age groups

For younger students

For preschool and early elementary students, you can do the activity in the following way:

1. Introduce the zones and tell students they will be using a book to help them learn how they can use zones to describe how they feel.
2. Using the book *On Monday When It Rained* or *The Way I Feel,* read to the students each description of how the character feels.
3. Before you reveal the character's emotion, have students guess the emotion and which zone the character is in.
4. As you read the book, have students glue each relevant emotion/state picture from Reproducible C onto the wall posters of the zones in the corresponding zone (for example: silly—yellow, scared—yellow, disappointed—yellow or blue, happy—green, sad—blue, angry—red, thankful—green, frustrated—yellow, shy—yellow or blue, bored—blue, excited—yellow, jealous—yellow or red, proud—green).
5. Ask the students about a time they felt each of these emotions and assess their ability to identify emotions in themselves. After the book is finished, reiterate that it is okay that students are in different zones at different times; this is expected and part of being who we are.

For older students

For upper elementary to high school students, you can do the activity in the following way:

1. Have students take turns selecting a picture from the container. When it is a student's turn, that student should tell the other students what the emotion is and also show them the picture (often students need prompting to address the class rather than face the wall posters). If the emotion is less familiar to the students, provide examples of when one may experience the emotion (for example, sometimes I feel *anxious* before a test).
2. Ask the student who chose the emotion to demonstrate to the class which facial expression correlates with the emotion.
3. As a group, discuss where to glue the picture within the zones. (Informally assess which students are grasping the concept of the zones through this task versus those who are not. Provide more support to students who are having a more difficult time.)
4. Have the student who drew the picture glue it to the poster in the zone decided on by the group.
5. Once completed, visually display the posters for the students to continue to view, such as on an uncluttered wall in the classroom at students' eye

level. Refer to the posters frequently after you do this lesson to aid the students in checking in and learning the zones.

Wrap-up

Assess students' abilities to recognize their zones at the end of the lesson by having the students state how they feel at the present time and asking them to identify their zone (see Check-In on page 96). Lead a discussion to further evaluate understanding by asking the following:

- *How will sorting the ways you feel and act into four zones help you understand yourself better?*
- *How will it help you understand your classmates better?*

Emphasize that when they understand how they are feeling, they are better able to control themselves. For example, when they recognize that they feel restless or frustrated, they are able to do something about it. Even if they don't have the tools to do something about it, at least they can tell others how they feel using a common language: The Zones of Regulation.

Ways to generalize learning

- Share with other team members, parents, and staff the Information About The Zones of Regulation and The Zones of Regulation Glossary (Reproducibles A and B).
- Teach regular education students about the zones and implement the language school wide.
- Talk aloud about your fluctuating zones.
- Post zones posters in places where students spend a lot of time (cafeteria, classroom, lunchroom).
- Send home with each student a copy of The Zones of Regulation Visual (see Reproducible E) so students and parents have a visual reference to talk about.
- Copies of The Zones of Regulation Visual (Reproducible E) can also be posted in areas the students frequent.

Additional learning activity for Lesson 1

Explain to students that they will act out the different zones while their classmates guess what zone they are in. Put paper squares cut out of the four zone colors into the container and have one student at a time discreetly draw one of the colors. Have that student then act like someone who is in that zone (provide an example of an emotion if necessary). When other students know what zone the student is acting out, have them raise their hands. The student actor calls on one of them to share the zone with the class. Gauge students' learning by their ability to act out the different zones correctly and their ability to identify the zones their classmates act out.

Blue

Hurt

Sad

Depressed

Tired

Sick

Bored

Exhausted

Shy

Green

Good

Calm

Appreciated

Proud

Thankful

Happy

Good Listener

Ready to Learn

Focused

Okay

Relaxed

Content

Yellow
Excited
Frustrated
Nervous
Anxious/Worried
Silly
Annoyed
Overwhelmed
Scared
Jealous
Upset
Uncomfortable
Confused
Embarrassed
Grouchy/Crabby

Red

Mean

Mad

Yelling

Angry

Aggressive

Terrified

Out of Control

Elated

BLUE ZONE

GREEN ZONE

YELLOW ZONE

RED ZONE

The ZONES

of Regulation®

The ZONES of Regulation®

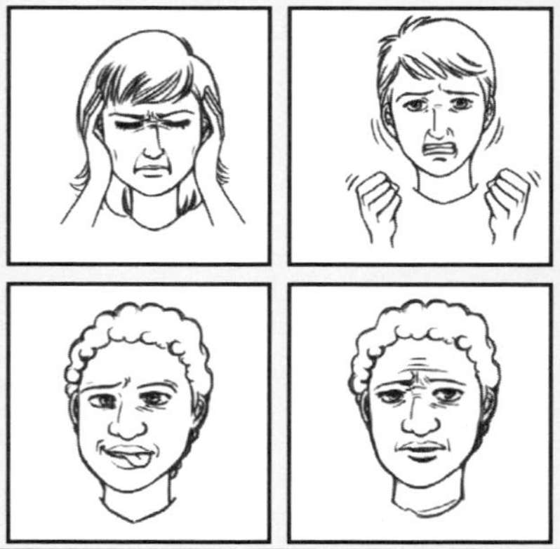

BLUE ZONE	GREEN ZONE	YELLOW ZONE	RED ZONE
Sad	Happy	Frustrated	Mad/Angry
Sick	Calm	Worried	Terrified
Tired	Feeling Okay	Silly/Wiggly	Yelling/Hitting
Bored	Focused	Excited	Elated
Moving Slowly	Ready to Learn	Loss of Some Control	Out of Control

Lesson 2:
Zones Bingo

Overview

In this activity, students play bingo while they practice displaying and guessing the meaning of each other's facial expressions. This lesson is designed to offer students an enjoyable way to further work on recognizing different emotions and expand their emotions vocabulary. This lesson also provides you with an informal opportunity to see if students are able to accurately categorize the emotions into the respective zones.

Goals for this activity

- Student increase their vocabulary of emotions
- Students increase their recognition of facial expressions
- Students deepen their understanding of the zones

Materials

- ☐ Bingo markers; for example, daubers (special markers in different colors used for marking off bingo cards), construction paper squares, poker chips, pennies, etc. If possible, use markers in the four zone colors.
- ☐ Paper cutter or scissors
- ☐ Zones Bingo Cards (see Reproducible F), one card per student
- ☐ One copy of Zones Emotions (see Reproducible C)
- ☐ A container in which to put the Zones Emotions, such as a hat, jar, or bucket

Note to teacher: Displaying a variety of facial expressions can be difficult for many students who have challenges in self-regulation because their affect is often flatter and less animated than that of their peers.

Preparation

- If needed, make bingo markers for the students to use with their Zones Bingo Cards by cutting up a sheet of construction paper into 1" squares.
- Copy one Zones Bingo Card (see "Materials") for each student.
- Copy one set of Zones Emotions from Reproducible C, and then cut out each emotion picture and place them in the container.
- Distribute one Zones Bingo Card and a set of bingo markers to each student.
- Write the schedule on the board:
  1. Lead-in
  2. Zones bingo
  3. Wrap-up

Lead-in

1. Start off by making a dramatic facial expression and ask the students to guess how you are feeling. Continue to demonstrate different expressions, asking the students to guess what you are feeling until you can stump them.
2. Ask the students the following question:

   Why is it important to know what someone's facial expression means?

   Explain to the students how important it is to read facial expressions so they are better able to tell what other people are thinking and feeling. A facial expression gives a clue to what other people may be thinking so that we can adjust how we are acting based on that information.
3. Share with students the goals of the activity.

Activity

1. Explain to the students that they will play Zones bingo to practice recognizing facial expressions and to discover new emotions.
2. Call out names of emotions and allow students time to find the corresponding picture of the facial expression that matches the emotion. If bingo markers are available in each of the zone colors, have students mark the emotion with the corresponding color.
   Note to teacher: If any students have difficulty finding the emotion, have another student demonstrate what the facial expression looks like.
3. You can assess student learning by seeing if they correctly match the emotion to the picture on their bingo card.
4. Have students continue to mark the pictures until a bingo is called. To check accuracy, have that student read back the emotions and identify into which zone each emotion falls.

Wrap-up

Conclude by asking students the following questions to assess learning through discussion:

- What new emotion or facial expression have you learned?
- Can you demonstrate it?
- Can you recognize what zone students or teachers are in by their facial expressions?
- How could reading someone's facial expression change how you interact with that person?

Emphasize again that a facial expression is a clue to what a person is thinking or feeling. When you can read what others are thinking, you can adjust your actions. Provide an example for the students by making a worried facial expression and asking the students how they would react. Invite other students to make facial expressions and continue to have their classmates reply how they would react.

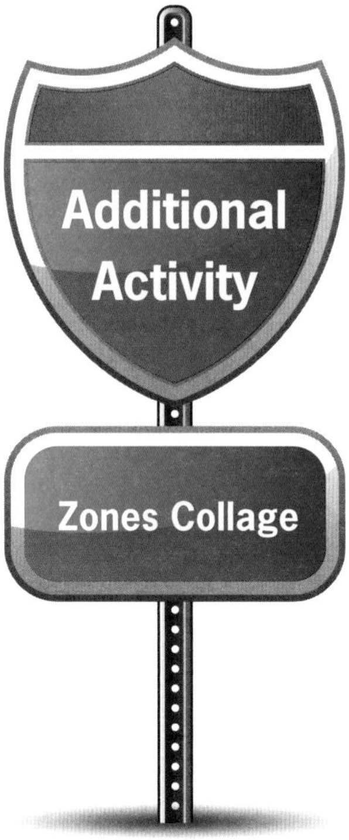

Ways to generalize learning

- Ask students throughout the week to make guesses about what zone people they observe are in based on each person's facial expression.
- Have students practice in a mirror making different facial expressions that match different emotions. This can be done at home during grooming activities with parents.

Additional learning activity for Lesson 2

Zones Collage (Idea contributed by Estelle Garcia)

Have the students look through magazines and cut out examples of people experiencing different emotions. Provide each student with a copy of the Zone Labels (Reproducible D), and ask them to glue each label onto construction paper with the corresponding color. Have students sort the pictures from the magazine that they cut out into the four zones. You can assess students' understanding of the zones and facial expressions by seeing if they sort the pictures onto the corresponding zones. Once checked for accuracy, have students glue the pictures into the zones. For further reinforcement, have students write the emotion the person is showing next to each picture. Display collages where students can continue to refer to them.

ZONES Bingo

ZONES Bingo

ZONES Bingo

ZONES Bingo

ZONES Bingo

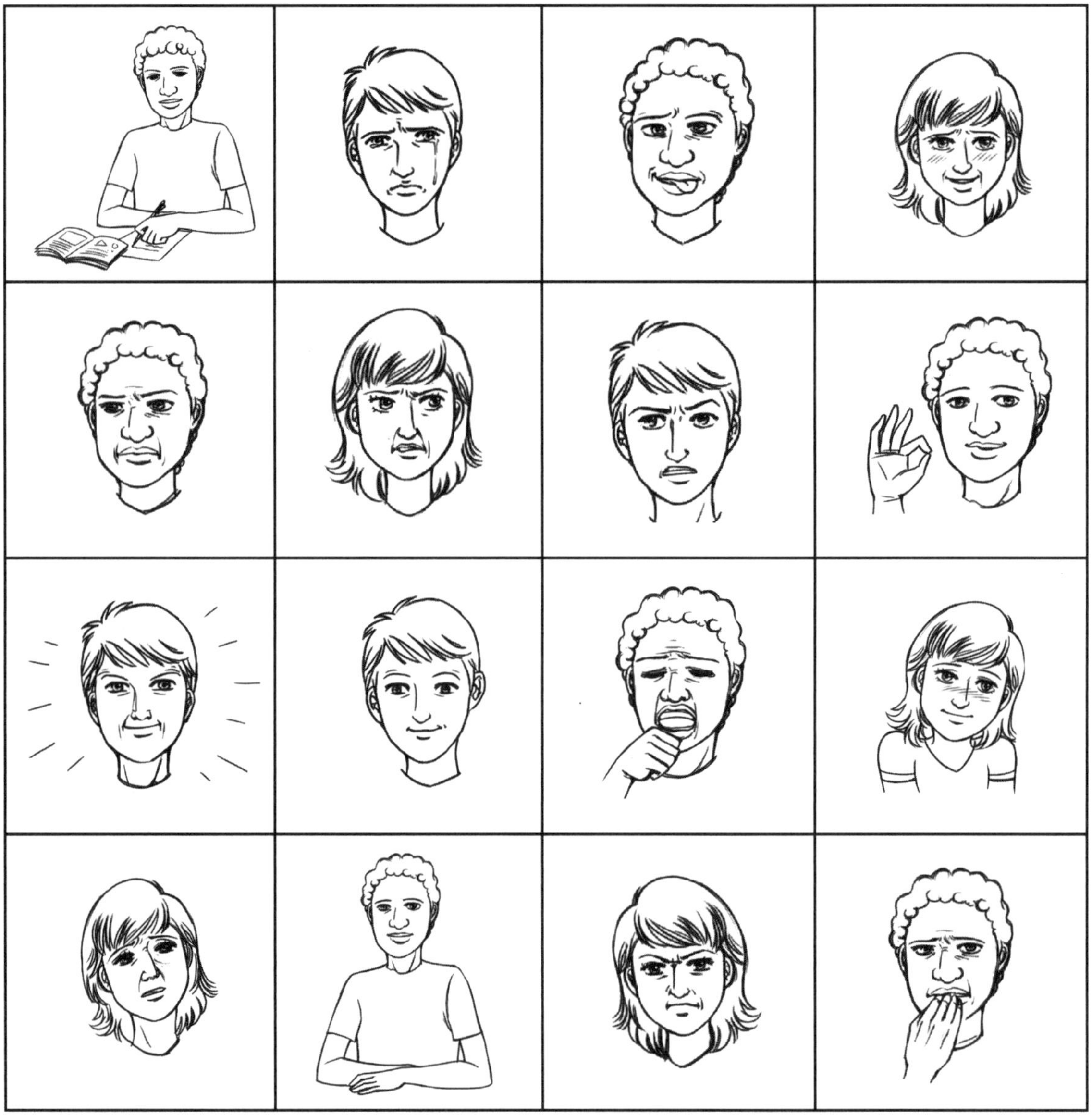

ZONES Bingo

ZONES Bingo

ZONES Bingo

Time for Refueling

Before You Begin the Next Lessons

As discussed in Chapter 1, Social Thinking® vocabulary (www.socialthinking.com) coined by Michelle Garcia Winner is integrated into The Zones vocabulary to help students understand how their behavior impacts others' thoughts and feelings. Before you continue further with The Zones lessons, introduce the following Social Thinking concepts and vocabulary to the students.

- "Expected" versus "unexpected" behavior
- "You can change/affect how I feel"
- "Good thoughts" versus "uncomfortable thoughts"

For ideas about how to introduce and reinforce these Social Thinking vocabulary terms, you can use the lessons (which have been slightly modified for use with The Zones) that are included here from Michelle Garcia Winner's curriculum *Think Social!* (2005). These Social Thinking concepts are important to teach students before they move to the next Zones lesson, as the vocabulary is infused throughout subsequent Zones learning activities.

Lesson: Expected and Unexpected Behavior[3]

This informs students that people actually notice other people's behavior and recognize whether they are abiding by the unwritten social rules or hidden rules.

How to use this lesson in the classroom

1. Give the students free time when they first come into the room. Videotape them playing (3–4 minutes).
   a. Encourage the students to join together in a group. Sit with the students in a circle on the floor (preferred) but a table is okay.

2. Observe who is looking like he or she is ready to be part of the group.

3. You, the teacher, will now perform a series of socially bizarre or unexpected behaviors while you talk to the group.

Critical Vocabulary

Expected behaviors

Unexpected behaviors

3. Adapted with permission from Winner's *Think Social!* (2005), page 36

   a. Lie down on the floor, or have your body turned out of the group or splayed across the worktable.
   b. Begin to talk to the students about learning how to be part of a group. Talk to them as if nothing unexpected is happening.
   c. Observe the students' reactions. If they look puzzled or start to ask you what you are doing, just let them continue to ask. Ignore their weird looks.

4. After a few minutes, ask the students if they think there is anything wrong or odd with the way you are behaving.
   a. Allow the students to tell you how they feel about you doing these unexpected behaviors.
   b. Encourage them to talk about what you are doing "wrong."
   c. Verbally praise them for figuring out that this behavior is unexpected and it makes them feel "nervous" or "uncomfortable."

5. On the blackboard, draw two columns. At the top of one column, write the words "Expected Behavior" and at the top of the other column write the words "Unexpected Behavior." If the students are too young to read, then draw a happy face in one column and an unhappy face in the other column.
   a. Using the students' feedback, make a list of what behaviors they might expect of you and the others who are in the group.
   b. Now make a list of behaviors that are unexpected. For younger students, draw sample pictures to illustrate the concepts.

6. Foster discussion about what students are expected to do with the following body parts if they are in the Green Zone:
   a. Eyes
   b. Head
   c. Shoulders
   d. Legs
   e. Hands

7. Acknowledge the students for sharing what they know about being in the group. Work with them on how "smart" they are for being aware of what makes people feel safe within groups of other people.

Use vocabulary that is appropriate to their age and current jargon such as *"cool," "awesome,"* etc.

Critical Vocabulary

"You can change (impact/affect) my feelings."

Lesson: Our Behavior Impacts the Feelings of Those Around Us[4]

You can now talk about the fact that when you see students doing expected behaviors it makes you feel more positive (proud, happy, etc.). You can also explicitly make the connection that when you see a student doing what is unexpected, this makes you feel more negative (frustrated, uncomfortable, angry, etc.). To have this lesson be effective, you MUST emphasize observing and talking about students who are doing what is expected or justified in the situation. Students are more likely to work towards making others feel good when they are aware of their own impact, even if they won't admit it.

How to use this lesson in the classroom

1. Use a poster or pictures (such as a printout of Zones Emotions—Reproducible C) that show various emotions to help students think of "feeling" words.

2. Discuss the fact that all people have feelings. Explain that even right now, while in the group, the students have reactions and feelings about the room, the people, and the lesson.

3. List emotion words describing how the students feel when you or they are doing what is expected (e.g., safe, good, happy).

4. List emotion words about how students feel when you or they are doing what is unexpected (e.g., yucky, bad, sad, mixed up).

5. Discuss that people's feelings can be changed by the behavior of others around them. Read aloud a passage or story where people's behavior changes based on how they feel. One example is *Miss Nelson Is Missing* (1977). In this book a teacher is frustrated by the behavior of the students in her classroom so she comes back disguised as a witch. This subsequently impacts how the children behave, and once they start to follow the rules, Miss Nelson (the teacher) returns.

6. What books can you think of that provide examples of how one's behavior impacts another's feelings? Discuss the connections between behavior and feelings.

7. Use the concept "you can change (impact/affect) my feelings." For younger children, address the simple concept that "you can change my feelings." For older students, use more sophisticated terminology by saying "you can impact or affect my feelings." Identify students whose recent behaviors give you a positive reaction/feeling. Identify students

4. Adapted with permission from Winner's *Think Social!* (2005), page 40

whose recent behavior gives you negative reactions/feelings. For example, you feel worried that a student is not working with the group, and this can even make you feel frustrated because it does not appear that he or she is listening.

8. If the student replies by saying he or she was listening, and then proceeds to tell you everything you just said, point out that it was great that the student was listening but that when you observed that the student was distracted, you FELT like he or she was not listening. Explain that the student's behavior caused a change in your own emotions. It is always important to get the idea across that your feelings are very real to you, even if the other person felt that you were not correct in feeling in the first place!

Lesson: Good Thoughts vs. Uncomfortable Thoughts[5]

Each of us has many thoughts about the different people at school, in the community, and even at home. This means we all have to be aware that others have thoughts about us as well—even when we are not talking to them! Many of the thoughts people have about us are appropriate thoughts or good thoughts. But all of us, at times, can cause other people to have uncomfortable thoughts about us. This is often the case when the zone we are in is unexpected.

Have students observe some other students at school. Who did they have "good thoughts" about? Why were their thoughts good (e.g., kids were following directions, sharing, etc.)? Who did they have uncomfortable thoughts about? Did the zone the student was in change the types of thoughts they had?

Encourage the students to discuss what behaviors and words cause us or others to have an "uncomfortable thought."

Critical Vocabulary

Good thoughts

Uncomfortable thoughts

How to use this lesson in the classroom

1. First, review this important concept with students: Each one of us can make people have good thoughts and uncomfortable thoughts about us by the way we behave. But when others have too many uncomfortable thoughts about us, they may think that we are not fun, safe, or easy to play or work with.

2. Visually demonstrate to students how their behaviors generate different types of thoughts in others (uncomfortable thoughts/good thoughts). Demonstrate this through the use of two different colored Popsicle sticks, paper clips, or any other small colored objects you have. The

5. Adapted with permission from Winner's *Think Social!* (2005), page 93

use of visual objects makes this social concept more understandable for students.

a. Provide each student with a set of objects that are two different colors (for example, purple Popsicle sticks and orange Popsicle sticks). You can use any two colors you choose; just keep your colors consistent over time.
b. Give a transparent cup to each child in the group. Reserve one for yourself. The cups sit in front of each person.
c. The sticks (or other items) represent what you, the educator, think about the student's behavior. A purple stick represents a "good thought" you are having about the student and an orange stick represents an "uncomfortable thought" you are having about the student.
d. When a student is working as part of the group and is doing expected behaviors that are generating good thoughts about him or her (e.g., waiting for others to speak, sitting patiently at the table, and establishing good physical presence), put a purple stick into his or her cup. Initially tell the student: "The purple thoughts are for the good thoughts I am having about you."
e. Once you have established the purpose of the purple stick, then you can silently acknowledge a person's good behavior by dropping a purple stick into his or her cup without having to say anything to the student. If it is not disruptive to the student, occasionally tell him or her what social behavior you observed that merits receiving another purple stick. It is especially important to acknowledge new emerging skills.
f. When the student exhibits a "negative" behavior, give him or her an orange stick. Describe the behavior and let the student know that the behavior made other people have an uncomfortable thought (e.g., "your eyes were not thinking about the people in the group," "your body was not in the group," "you said words that caused others to feel sad"). Again, be concise when placing the stick in the cup once students understand the meaning of the sticks.
g. Avoid giving only orange sticks to a child. It is important to realize that the orange sticks are ONLY significant if the child has accumulated a series of purple sticks! Most students, even difficult ones, exhibit many "purple stick" behaviors, but we often forget to give them credit for doing what we expect them to do. We pay more attention to their "orange stick" behaviors. For the lesson to succeed, you must actively pay attention to the "purple stick" behaviors and give select attention to the "orange stick" behaviors.

You must find the opportunity to give students plenty of purple sticks to motivate them to reduce their "orange stick" behaviors.

3. Make a list of expected behaviors that earn purple sticks. The opposite—or absence—of purple stick behaviors is what constitutes orange stick behaviors.

4. You can use the visual information represented by the sticks to help students understand why other students choose to work with some kids and not others. The students with too many orange sticks may not be seen as "safe" (fun, easy, etc.) to be with because their behavior is less predictable. The sticks also motivate students to monitor their social behavior more closely as they serve as a mild reward system.

5. Students will ask to have you remove their orange sticks once they repair their behavior. Do not remove a student's orange stick yourself. Instead, explain that the student can take the orange stick out of the cup, he or she can even break it, but what the student can't do is take it out of your memory. The sticks in the cup represent your thoughts and your thoughts help to form your memory.

6. However, the student can make the orange sticks appear to go away by earning more purple sticks. This makes it difficult to even see the orange sticks in the cup, thus visually underscoring the idea that good thoughts overtake any uncomfortable thoughts that might be in your memory. This is an important behavioral concept we need to introduce and then reinforce; behavior can be modified and plenty of good thoughts help to minimize the power of uncomfortable thoughts we have about people.

Lesson 3:
The Zones in Video

Goals for this activity

- Students deepen their understanding of The Zones of Regulation and learn to identify the zones in others
- Students gain awareness of how others perceive people in the different zones
- Students learn that one's behavior can change/affect others' feelings and zones
- Students observe movie or television characters' social skills and gain insight into expected and unexpected behaviors

Materials

- ☐ TV with a VCR or DVD player or a computer that can play DVDs or downloaded movies or shows
- ☐ Movie, sitcom episode, or cartoon in which characters display many states of alertness and emotions
  Recommended movies:
  For older students: *The Outsiders* (Zoetrope Studios)
  For younger students:
  Charlie Brown films or
  TV specials by Charles Schultz or
  Finding Nemo by Disney
  It's great to use video clips with which you are already familiar. Avoid using movies or shows that the students are obsessed with so that they can stay focused on emotions, facial expressions, etc.
  It is critical that you prescreen all media clips to avoid showing clips with inappropriate language or situations.
- ☐ A set of Popsicle craft sticks or cards in the four colors of zones for each student

Overview

In this activity, students view video clips and identify zones in the characters who are portrayed. It is intended to help students become more skilled in identifying emotions and zones in other people. It also allows students to grasp that everyone experiences the different zones; it's not just them. You can also use the clips to point out how one character's behavior is viewed by others to teach viewing things from different perspectives and the concept of expected and unexpected behavior. Before students can correctly identify the zones in themselves, they must be able to recognize the zones in others.

Preparation

Now that you are prepared to integrate the above strategies, you can get ready to do this video activity with students.

- Cue up the movie or TV show episode and distribute one set of color-coded sticks or cards to each student.
- Write the schedule on the board:
  1. Lead-in
  2. Watch show (pausing several times)
  3. Wrap-up

Lead-in

1. Elicit the students' insights into their awareness of their own behaviors around others by asking:
   Have you ever considered how the zone you are in can impact other people who are nearby?
2. Review the goals of the activity with the students.

Activity

1. Explain to students that they will watch a part of a movie or show that you will pause numerous times to discuss what zone the different characters are in.
2. Start playing the video. Each time you pause the playback, ask the students to raise the colored stick or card that represents the appropriate zone. Evaluate if students are able to correctly identify people in the different zones by observing if they hold up the correct color. If there is no consensus among the colors raised, open a discussion on why the students raised the different colors. Through dialogue, see if students

present good arguments to back their color choice. Check for understanding and clear up misconceptions.

3. When appropriate during the show, pause the video and raise questions to allow students the opportunity to reflect on the behavior of the characters:
   - *What kind of thoughts do others have when the character is in the Red Zone ("good thoughts" vs. "uncomfortable thoughts")?*
   - *How do others react to the character?*
   - *Is the way he or she acts when in the Yellow Zone "expected" for the situation?*
   - *Is the character able to interact with others as successfully when he or she is in the Red or Yellow Zone as when the character is in the Green Zone?*
4. Point out an "unexpected" behavior and how it changed the way others felt (or how it changed their zone).

Wrap-up

Once your group has watched the portion of the movie or episode, lead the class in a discussion using the following questions to assess understanding:

- *How did the characters get along with each other when they were in the different zones?*
- *What were others thinking about them when they were in the Yellow or Red Zone and it was unexpected?*
- *In which zone were the characters most successful?*
- *What did people think of them when their zone was expected?*
- *In what zone do you feel you get along best with others or are most successful?*

If students don't point it out, stress that the characters were more likely to have positive interactions when they were in the Green Zone. Emphasize that they can perform better when they can remain calm and focused. Talk to students about how other people may perceive their behavior as disruptive or inappropriate in the Yellow Zone, even though *they* (the students) may not.

Lesson 4:
The Zones in Me

Overview

In this activity, students decide what would be the expected zone for a variety of scenarios. Younger students express what zone is the expected response by jumping into an area marked for that zone on the floor; older students discuss what they think and note the zone on a worksheet. Both age groups complete a worksheet to determine the expected zone for a given situation. With this activity, students explore the concept that all of the zones are expected under different circumstances, and it is okay to experience all of them. This activity helps students reflect on how different experiences affect the zone they are in; for example, if students do not get the grade they expected on a test, that may put them in the Yellow Zone.

Goals for this activity

- Students learn to identify the zones in themselves
- Students learn it is natural and expected to experience all of the zones in different situations/environments
- Students increase their awareness of how external factors, such as who is near them and where they are, impact what zone is expected
- Students reflect on the positive and negative impacts of matching their zone to the demands of the environment/situation

Materials

- ☐ One copy of Zones Scenarios (Reproducible G)
- ☐ One copy of Which Zone Should I Be In? (Reproducible H) for each student (worksheet idea contributed by Jill Kuzma; http://jillkuzma.wordpress.com)
- ☐ A container, such as a hat, bucket, or jar, from which to draw scenarios
- ☐ **For younger students (preschool and early elementary):** Hula hoops, spots, or other objects to place on the floor to represent the four zone colors

Preparation

- Cut apart the Zones Scenarios and place them in the container.
- Customize additional scenarios that are specific to the students with whom you are working. Zones Scenarios (Reproducible G) includes empty boxes for this purpose.
- If you are using the activity with younger students, place the objects on the floor to represent the four zone colors. Place them closely together in a square so students can jump between "zones."
- Review the Social Thinking vocabulary previously introduced:
  - "Expected" versus "unexpected" behavior
  - "You can change/affect how I feel"
  - "Good thoughts" versus "uncomfortable thoughts"
- Write the schedule on the board:
  1. Lead-in
  2. Zones activity (for younger students only)
  3. Which Zone Should I Be In? worksheet
  4. Wrap-up

Lead-in for all ages

1. Elicit the students' insights into their self-awareness of circumstances when they were in each of the zones by asking:

   Tell me about a time this week when you were in the Blue Zone? Green Zone? Yellow Zone? Red Zone?

Note to teacher: This may be very difficult for some students, so it's not recommended that you push if students aren't ready to talk about it. Having insight into the students' zones from parents or teachers is helpful if you are unsure of specific circumstances.

2. Review what they will do in the activity and its goals with the students. With younger students, point out the zones on the floor that they will jump to during the activity. Younger students may need more examples, such as, "you were really mad at your friend for not sharing" or "you couldn't wait your turn to hold the caterpillar because you were SO EXCITED"

Activities for different age groups

1. Draw scenarios from the container and read them to the students.
2. After each scenario, have students determine which zone they think is expected for that zone.

   If you're doing the activity with younger students (preschool through early elementary): This activity can be done individually or in groups of two or more. When working with two or more students, have students take turns. When it is a student's turn, he or she jumps into the zone expected for that scenario. Record the students' answers on the Which Zone Should I Be In? worksheet.

   If you're doing the activity with older students (upper elementary through high school): Give each student one copy of the worksheet before you begin. Instead of jumping into a zone, have students take turns drawing and reading the scenario aloud to the group. Have the student express which zone he or she thinks is expected and then facilitate a discussion with the other students to get group consensus. Have students record their decisions on the Which Zone Should I Be In? worksheet.

3. If you have not already done so, give each student the Which Zone Should I Be In? worksheet to fill out. You can have each student complete the worksheet individually or you can do this activity as a group as part of a discussion about in which circumstances it is expected that someone would be in the four different zones. For example, they could discuss how the Red Zone is expected if you get devastating news, there is an emergency situation or disaster, or you get physically injured. This worksheet can also be sent home to do with parents as homework. Younger students will need assistance with the writing demands and scribing for them would be appropriate.

Wrap-up

After students complete the activity, lead the class in a discussion using the following questions to assess understanding:

Are there times when it is expected to be in a zone other than green?
Describe a circumstance when you were in a zone other than green.
Was it expected or unexpected? How could you tell?

Note to Teacher

Students may jump into or identify a zone that may be unexpected for the given circumstance. For example, when you read the scenario "You were told that the plans need to change," students might jump in the Red Zone. If this happens, you can ask them if the Red Zone is expected given that scenario and if people will have good or uncomfortable thoughts of the person who is in the Red Zone. Another example is if the plan was to go to Disneyland and they are no longer going, the Yellow Zone may be expected. However, if the plan was to go to the library and then the store, and they end up only having time to go to the store, the Red Zone would be unexpected.

It is important to teach that there is no "naughty" zone, but sometimes behaviors in a zone may be unexpected given the environment they are in or who they are with.

It is important to stress that all of the zones are okay and expected given different circumstances. Discuss times when it is expected to be in the Blue (on a rainy day), Yellow (startled by the loud fire drill at school), and Red Zones (getting in a car accident). Also highlight that sometimes the behaviors typically seen in a zone are unexpected given the circumstance, leading those around you to have uncomfortable thoughts about you. Emphasize that they can perform better in the classroom if they can remain calm and focused in the Green Zone.

Ways to generalize learning

- Copy the completed Which Zone Should I Be In? worksheet for each student and share it with others who work closely with the student, including parents.
- While watching TV shows or movies or reading literature, ask parents to reinforce learning by having students determine if a character's zone was expected or unexpected given the situation.

Additional learning activity for Lesson 4

Lights, Camera, Action

A video camera can be used for a variety of purposes (make sure you have parental permission to videotape for educational purposes). If students are having difficulty recognizing their zone, videotape a segment of their day, making sure there is a lot of positive footage. Review the footage with the students, pausing when they are in the different zones so the students can reflect on how they look and feel in that zone. The footage can also be used to help students learn how *others* respond to *them* when they are in the different zones and how the student's zone can change/affect the way others feel. Footage taken of the class can be played back to the students. If this causes discomfort for a student, accommodate by playing back the footage in a one-to-one setting. By using color-coded Popsicle sticks, the students can work on identifying the zones in themselves as well as their peers. You can pose questions similar to those in "Wrap-up" to check for understanding.

ZONES Scenarios

Your parent tells you that someone close to you passed away.	You turn on the TV and find out a war has broken out.	You experience a natural disaster (large earthquake, tornado, flood, hurricane).
You break your leg in P.E. class.	You are playing a competitive game.	You found out that you won the lottery.
You are playing tag on the playground with friends.	You are participating in the class discussion.	You are listening to a teacher give instructions.
You just woke up in the morning.	You are home with nothing to do.	You can't find your assignment you worked hard on.

ZONES Scenarios

You are working with a partner on a science project.	You are playing/ hanging out with a friend at the friend's house.	You didn't do well on a test.
You were told that the plans need to change.	You are asked to stop or put away something that you enjoy doing.	You have been waiting for more than 30 minutes at the doctor's office.
You are sitting with your family at the dinner table.	Your pet is missing.	You got the flu.
You just ran a mile as fast as you could.		

Which ZONE Should I Be In?

All of the zone colors are okay. There are times when you should be in different zones. In the classroom, we try to stay in the Green Zone. Think about times when it's expected that you would be in the Yellow, Blue, or even the Red Zone.

Times when it is expected to be in each zone...

Times to be in the BLUE ZONE...

Times to be in the GREEN ZONE...

Times to be in the YELLOW ZONE...

Times to be in the RED ZONE...

Lesson 5:
Understanding Different Perspectives

Goals for this activity

- Students gain awareness of how others perceive them in the different zones
- Students learn that their behavior can change and affect others' thoughts, feelings, and zones
- Students reflect on the positive and negative impacts of matching their zone to the demands of the environment and situation

Materials

For younger students (preschool and early elementary)

- ☐ One copy of Understanding Different Perspectives (Reproducible I) for each student (worksheet idea contributed by Jill Kuzma; http://jillkuzma.wordpress.com)

For older students (upper elementary through high school)

- ☐ One copy of the Expected Social Behavior Map and the Unexpected Social Behavior Map (Reproducible J and Reproducible K) for each student
- ☐ Dry erase markers and board

Overview

In this activity, students reflect on how others are viewing their behavior through the completion of worksheets if they are younger or a Social Behavior Map™ if they are third grade or older (see description and instructions below). Social Behavior Mapping was developed by Michelle Garcia Winner (Winner, 2007; www.socialthinking.com). By using the worksheets or Social Behavior Maps to facilitate discussions, students gain skills in viewing others' perspectives and understanding how consequences are linked to how people feel about their behavior, helping them to see the bigger picture of their role in social interaction. As social beings, we are motivated to behave according to what we think will keep those around us thinking positive thoughts of us. We are able to understand that others have different thoughts and feelings and so we are socially driven to take into account others' perspectives to help us regulate our actions. Students who struggle with self-regulation often have an impaired ability to consider others' perspectives and subsequently aren't motivated by social expectations to help them regulate. Therefore, they need to learn how to take others' perspectives into account so that they can become more effective regulators.

Caution

Cautionary note: Not all students with social learning challenges efficiently understand that their own thoughts are different from others' thoughts. That means it will be difficult to proceed with teaching lessons of social-emotional perspective taking if your student doesn't have this social knowledge. If your student appears to lack this information, please focus on lessons presented earlier in the book as well as on exploring sensory supports and calming tools (see Lessons 10, 11, 13, and 18). You can Google the concept "Theory of Mind" to learn more about this area of functioning.

Preparation

- Print one copy of Reproducible I or of Reproducibles J and K for each student, depending on students' grade level.
- Write the schedule on the board:
  1. Lead-in
  2. Understanding different perspectives activity
  3. Wrap-up

Lead-in for all ages

1. Elicit the students' insights into their self-awareness and ask how they affect others:
   Have you ever considered how the zone you are in can impact the way others think and feel about you?
2. Review the goals of the activity with the students.

Activities for different age groups

For younger students

For preschool and early elementary students, you can do the activity in the following way:

> Work with students to fill out the worksheets on Understanding Different Perspectives. If you know about a circumstance when a student was in a zone, you can use it to trigger them to think about how others were impacted. You may find it easier or necessary to act as a scribe for them.

For older students (third grade and above)—introducing a Social Behavior Map

For upper elementary through high school students, you can do the learning activity by having students complete a Social Behavior Map (SBM) together. See Figure 3 and the Social Behavior Mapping templates (Reproducibles J, K).

Figure 3:
Examples of Social Behavior Mapping[6]

The **ZONES** of Regulation® Reproducible J[1] (Example)

Social Behavior Mapping
What's Expected for:
Being in the Green Zone in the Classroom

Expected behaviors	How the behaviors make people FEEL	How people react to how THEY FEEL about your behavior	How the person feels about himself or herself
1. Attending to teacher, taking notes	Teacher feels respected	I get good grades from my teachers	Proud
2. Head up, looking at materials being presented.	Classmates feel comfortable around me	Positive reports at conferences	Good
3. Engaged in classroom discussion (raising hand, adding comments)	Others feel I am a good student	Classmates want to sit near me	Liked by others
4. Semi-upright posture, shoulders turned toward speaker		I get asked by classmates to work on projects together	Smarter

1 Social Behavior Mapping is the original work of Michelle Garcia Winner, *Thinking About YOU, Thinking About ME* (2007), pages 156–157 (www.socialthinking.com). Permission to reproduce Social Behavior Maps was granted by Michelle Garcia Winner.

The **ZONES** of Regulation® Reproducible K[1] (Example)

Social Behavior Mapping
What's Unexpected for:
Being in the Blue Zone in the Classroom

Unexpected behaviors	How the behaviors make people FEEL	How people react to how THEY FEEL about your behavior	How the person feels about himself or herself
1. Head down on the table, slumped posture	Classmates feel ignored	Teacher and classmates think I am rude	Lousy
2. Sleeping in class	Teacher feels disrespected	Students do not want to work with me on projects	Distant from others
3. Ignoring others when they talk to me	Teacher questions if he or she is a good teacher and wonders how to reach me	Poor performance on assignments and tests	Bored
4. Sitting away from others		Parents receive negative feedback from teachers	
5. Not thinking of others with my eyes		Other kids ignore me	
6. No participation in class discussions		Get a reputation as lazy, unmotivated, or dumb	

1 Social Behavior Mapping is the original work of Michelle Garcia Winner, *Thinking About YOU, Thinking About ME* (2007), pages 156–157 (www.socialthinking.com). Permission to reproduce Social Behavior Maps was granted by Michelle Garcia Winner.

6. Social Behavior Mapping is the original work of Michelle Garcia Winner, *Thinking About YOU, Thinking About ME* (2007), pages 156-7 (www.socialthinking.com). Permission to reproduce Social Behavior Maps was granted by Michelle Garcia Winner.

Social Behavior Map Instructions (from Michelle Garcia Winner)

When using the Social Behavior Map, start by completing the "expected" behaviors map (Reproducible J):

1. Write at the top of each SBM which behavioral set you are describing, (e.g., "Being in the Green Zone in the Classroom").
   a. List the "expected" set of behaviors in the left hand column (e.g., "calm body," "focused mind," "facing teacher, "quiet mouth/hands/feet").
   b. List how the student's behaviors make other people feel (taking their perspective). Use emotional words or phrases such as "pleased," "respected," or "happy that you (*the student)* are working as part of the group."
   c. List what consequences (generally the more positive ones) evolve from making people feel good about what the student is doing (e.g., "Get good grades," "asked to be a partner").
   d. List how the student ultimately feels about him or herself when he or she does the expected behaviors in the right hand column (e.g., "proud," "happy").

2. Do the same process now on the Unexpected page (Reproducible K), writing on top of the SBM what behavioral set you are describing, e.g., "Being in the Yellow Zone in the Classroom."

   a. List the unexpected behaviors to match the behavioral set you are defining (e.g., "blurts out in class," "gets out of his seat," "is easily frustrated by assigned work").
   b. List how these unexpected behaviors affect someone else's perspective by listing emotional words such as, "frustrated," "annoyed," or "worried that *student* is not learning."
   c. List the related consequences (e.g., "*Student's* teacher has a strict tone of voice when she tells him what he needs to do," "*Student* may be asked to leave the group or the room," "*Student* loses a point on his earning chart").
   d. List how the student ends up feeling about himself or herself, (e.g., "frustrated," "lonely").

Note to teacher from Michelle Garcia Winner: Educators have commented that it does not feel comfortable to tell a student that a particular behavior that he or she is engaging in affects the feelings of the adult or a peer. The important point to consider is that our reluctance to verbally acknowledge our feelings to others is based on the assumption that typical people can "read" us intuitively and thus they can regulate their behavior accordingly. The reality for many of our students is that they have true social-cognitive deficits impacting their ability to "read" how emotional states of others are connected to the behavioral actions

Note to Teacher

You can produce an Unexpected SBM for being in any zone (see Figure 3 for an example of a completed Unexpected SBM). Tailor the zone to meet students' needs. For example, if a student is predominantly in the Yellow Zone in the classroom and his peers and teachers find it uncomfortable, use "Being in the Yellow Zone in the Classroom" as the behavioral set for the Unexpected SBM.

of the student. Of course, this is not to say that there aren't times when one of our students engages in a malicious behavior with full awareness of how he is impacting other people. Although our students at times may be purposely misbehaving, at many other times those same students are doing an unexpected behavior with no awareness of how it was impacting others in their environment. While realizing that we try to be extremely positive when working out behavioral teaching plans, these students may have a difficult time knowing when they have done an "unexpected" behavior. By only attending to their positive behavior, we may not be giving them all the information they need to see the bigger picture of what they are doing.

Wrap-up

After the worksheets or behavior maps are complete, lead the class in a discussion using the following questions to assess understanding:

- *How do you get along with others when you are in the different zones?*
- *In which zone are you most successful?*
- *What kind of thoughts do people have when you are in the Green Zone?*
- *Are there times people may have uncomfortable thoughts about you if you are in the Green Zone?*

If students fail to point this out, stress that students have more successful interactions when they are in the Green Zone. Emphasize that they can perform better if they can remain calm and focused. Although students may not perceive their behavior as disruptive or inappropriate in the Yellow Zone, talk to them about how other people may see it in this way. Completed work can be stored in the students' Zones Folder.

Ways to generalize learning

- Review the worksheets or SBMs with the students' teams so that all can understand the language and consequences (it may be necessary to facilitate discussions with parents and other key players before completing the maps so everyone is on the same page).
- The worksheets and SBMs should be frequently reviewed with the students, allowing the students to reflect on their behaviors that are viewed both positively and negatively by others.
- Talk with the student about what zone is expected using a SBM before a student enters a situation that could potentially lead him or her to a less regulated state.

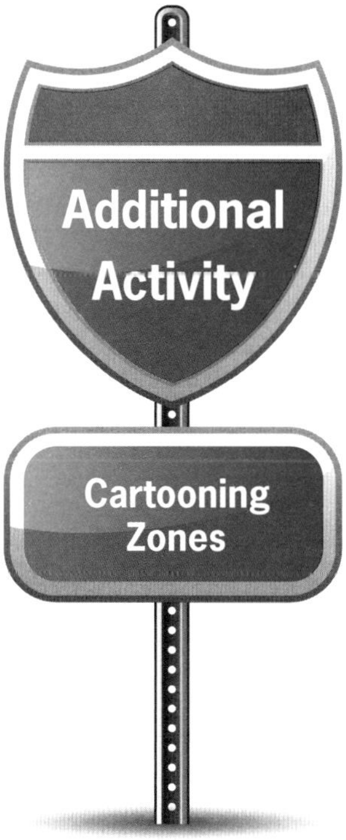

Additional learning activity for Lesson 5

Cartooning Zones

Complement the discussion by cartooning specific events that occurred where the student was in an unexpected zone. By creating comic book conversations (see *Comic Strip Conversations* by Carol Gray in "Recommended

Resources") of Yellow, Red, and Blue Zone behaviors, the students can visually see their peers' and teachers' perspectives via the thinking bubbles. Give students the option if they want to draw the cartoons or have you draw for them.

Refer to the second edition of Michelle Garcia Winner's books *Teach Social!* and *Thinking About YOU Thinking About ME* (see "Recommended Resources") for further information and lessons in the area of perspective taking.

Understanding Different Perspectives

When I am in the **BLUE ZONE** and it is unexpected...

Other kids might feel around me.

Other kids might be thinking or

Other kids might say or

Understanding Different Perspectives

When I am in the **GREEN ZONE** and it is expected...

Other kids might feel around me.

Other kids might be thinking

or

Other kids might say

or

Understanding Different Perspectives

When I am in the YELLOW ZONE and it is unexpected...

Other kids might feel around me.

Other kids might be thinking

or

Other kids might say

or

Understanding Different Perspectives

When I am in the **RED ZONE** and it is unexpected...

Other kids might feel ______ ______ around me.

Other kids might be thinking

or

Other kids might say

or

Social Behavior Mapping

What's Expected for: ______________________________

Expected behaviors	How your behaviors make people FEEL	How people react to how THEY FEEL about your behavior	How YOU FEEL about yourself based on how people react to you
1.			
2.			
3.			
4.			
5.			

1 Social Behavior Mapping is the original work of Michelle Garcia Winner, *Thinking About YOU, Thinking About ME* (2007), pages 156-157 (www.socialthinking.com). Permission to reproduce Social Behavior Maps was granted by Michelle Garcia Winner.

Social Behavior Mapping

What's Unexpected for: ____________________

Unexpected behaviors	How your behaviors make people FEEL	How people react to how THEY FEEL about your behavior	How YOU FEEL about yourself based on how people react to you
1.			
2.			
3.			
4.			
5.			

1 Social Behavior Mapping is the original work of Michelle Garcia Winner, *Thinking About YOU, Thinking About ME* (2007), pages 156-157 (www.socialthinking.com). Permission to reproduce Social Behavior Maps was granted by Michelle Garcia Winner.

Lesson 6:
Me in My Zones

Overview
In this activity, students draw or take photos of themselves in the different zones. This helps them gain insight into some of the physiological cues their bodies give them that let them know they are in the different zones. This in turn will help them increase their awareness of their zones and potentially give them more forewarning that they are becoming less regulated. Some students are described as going "straight from the Green Zone to the Red Zone." For each student, it is especially critical that time is spent exploring what the student's Yellow Zone looks like so that student becomes more vigilant of the signs that he or she is moving into this heightened state.

Goals for this activity
- Students gain an increased awareness of how they feel and look in each zone
- Students improve their ability to identify which zone they are in

Materials
- ☐ One Me in My Zones worksheet (Reproducible L) for each student
- ☐ Markers, crayons, or colored pencils (optional)
- ☐ Polaroid® or digital camera and related equipment for printing (computer, printer, and paper) (optional)
- ☐ Glue or tape
- ☐ Permanent thin point markers (if using photographs)

Preparation
- Staple the pages (except the last page) of the Me in My Zones worksheets together to form a packet for each student.
- From the last page of the worksheets, cut out and glue the labels on the corresponding pages to use the Me in My Zones packet as a visual for students to relate tools to each zone (see Lesson 12). Do this for each student packet. Create a visual of a finished product for the students to use as an example.
- Write on the board the different questions you want the students to think about for each picture:
  - Are your muscles relaxed or tense?
  - Is your breathing fast or slow?
  - Is your heart beating fast or slow?
  - Is your brain focused or cluttered?
  - What does your face look like?
  - What sort of words and voice volume are coming out of your mouth?
  - Other ideas you can point out include the following: flushed cheeks, mind racing, fidgety or can't sit still, slumped posture, head down, more sensitive to ________, pursed lips, furrowed eyebrows, etc.
- Write the schedule on the board:
  1. Lead-in
  2. Draw yourself in each of the zones **or** take pictures in each of the zones
  3. List your body's clues for each zone
  4. Wrap up

Lead-in

1. Engage students in discussion by asking the students the following question:

   Do you believe there are signs our body gives us that help us know which zone we are in?

   Talk about the different body signs written on the board, visually demonstrating them if possible. Ask students to think about and visualize which of these they experience. Stress that every student looks different in each zone.
2. Explain to students that in this activity they will draw a picture or take a photo of what they look like in each zone. Review with the students the goals for this learning activity.

> ### Note to Teacher
>
> If you're taking photographs, plan on filling some time while you print the photographs or divide the lesson into two sessions to allow time for printing.

Activity

1. Have students either draw a picture of what they look like in each zone or take photos of each student as they act like they are in each zone. If you have more than one camera, students can take pictures of each other in the different zones. Using a camera is particularly helpful for students who have difficulty drawing. Tell the students they will have time to reflect on the clues their bodies give per zone.
2. Have students list next to each picture their body's signs for that zone. (For photographs, they can use permanent marker to write on the photographs.) You may find it easier or necessary to act as a scribe for students.
3. You can evaluate students' abilities to recognize their bodies' signs by observing their drawings and listed clues. Ensure that each student's clues are authentic traits to them for each zone.

Wrap-up

Further assess students' insights by asking them to share one of their pictures with their peers. As a student is describing how he or she looks in the zone, assess if this is consistent with your observations of the student. To evaluate if students are able to connect the zones into meaningful applications, ask students the following:

How can it be helpful for you to know how to read your body in the different zones?

Why would it be helpful to tell others what zone you are in?

Provide examples and explain that by reading bodily cues, students will be able to catch themselves before they lose control. When students are able to notice they are in the Blue, Yellow, or Red Zone, they can react to their bodies' signs and change the direction they are heading (i.e., self-regulate their behavior). Stress how they can adjust their interaction with someone depending on that person's zone. You can use the following statement to reiterate the point:

If I know that you are in the Red Zone, I will keep my distance until you cool down. If I can see that you are in the Yellow Zone, I can be careful that I do not do anything to upset you and can help you figure out how to get back to the Green Zone. If I know that you are in the Blue Zone, I may understand why you are participating less that day and help you find ways to get yourself going. If I know that you are in the Green Zone, I can expect you will be actively involved in the lesson or conversation and ready to learn.

Have each student store the completed Me in My Zones packet in the Zones Folder.

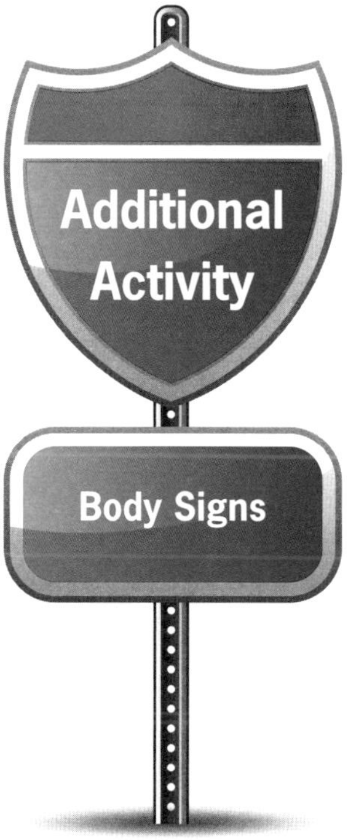

Ways to generalize learning

- In a variety of environments and situations, ask students what zone they are in.
- Have students share their Me in My Zones packets with parents and others with whom they work closely.
- Have students revisit their portraits in each of the zones after some time and see if they can add more details.

Additional learning activity for Lesson 6

Depending on the insightfulness of each student, direct feedback for students on their body signs will be helpful. You can capture video of the students in each zone to provide more feedback for reflection.

Me in My ZONES

Name: ______________________

This is a picture of me in the BLUE ZONE:

My face and body clues are:

→ ______________________

→ ______________________

→ ______________________

I feel in the BLUE ZONE when:

____

I am more likely to make others feel:

____

Name: ______________________

This is a picture of me in the GREEN ZONE:

My face and body clues are:

→ ______________________

→ ______________________

→ ______________________

I feel in the GREEN ZONE when:

____

I am more likely to make others feel:

____

Name: ______________________

This is a picture of me in the YELLOW ZONE:

My face and body clues are:

____

____

____

I feel in the YELLOW ZONE when:

____

I am more likely to make others feel:

____

Name: ______________________________

This is a picture of me in the RED ZONE:

My face and body clues are:

- ______________________________
- ______________________________
- ______________________________

I feel in the RED ZONE when:

____

I am more likely to make others feel:

____

Directions:

Staple all the pages together **except for this one.** Cut out and glue the headings below to the page opposite the picture of him or her in the corresponding colored zone. For example: When the book opens to *This is a picture of me in the Blue Zone* page, the heading on the left side page opposite it will be: *When I'm in the Blue Zone, I can try these Blue Zone tools* (tools are covered in lessons 10-12).

When I'm in the Blue Zone,
I can try these Blue Zone tools:

When I'm in the Green Zone,
I can try these Green Zone tools:

When I'm in the Yellow Zone,
I can try these Yellow Zone tools:

When I'm in the Red Zone,
I can try these Red Zone tools:

Lesson 7:
How Do I Feel?

Goals for this activity

- Students understand that different events change the way they are feeling
- Students improve their ability to use emotional vocabulary to describe how they are feeling
- Students are able to classify the feelings into the zones to demonstrate understanding of the zones concept

Materials

For younger students
(preschool through elementary school)

- ☐ *How Do I Feel? An Interactive Reading Book of Emotions* by Joan Green (see "Recommended Resources")

For older students
(middle school through high school)

- ☐ For middle and high school students, *I Have Feelings, Too! An Interactive Reading Book of Emotions for Teens, Adults and Seniors* by Joan Green (see "Recommended Resources")
  Note to teacher: The graphics in this book may be seen by some adolescents as childish.
- ☐ Four small sheets of construction paper, one in each color of the zones

Overview

In this activity, students match an emotion to a hypothetical scenario that is read from an interactive book about feelings and categorize the selected emotion into one of the four zones. This helps students further explore emotions and recognize how different events evoke a range of emotions. Often students report they are always in the Green Zone. This activity reinforces the concept that different events affect the way we feel and change the zone we are in. This activity is effective when working one-to-one with a student, given the personal reactions to different scenarios.

Preparation

- Obtain the appropriate book and have all Velcro pictures attached to the front pages. Arrange four sheets of construction paper on the table in the order of the zones.
- Write the schedule on the board:
  1. Lead-in
  2. Book activity
  3. Wrap-up

Lead-in

1. Explain to the students many things happen to us throughout the day that influence our zones, and use an example with which the students can identify:

   I notice that although a student may be in the Green Zone, if another student bumps into him or her, it seems to make him or her upset and puts that student in the Yellow Zone. Just a little thing like someone bumping into you can change what zone you are in within a second.

   Ask the students to think of examples of things that make them change zones.
2. Share with students what they will do and the goals of the lesson.

Activity

1. Inform the students that you will explore feelings and the different zones by using the book, *How Do I Feel?* or *I Have Feelings, Too!*
2. Begin with the students sorting all of the books' pictures onto the construction paper that represents the four zones (Figure 4). While the students complete this task, you can assess their understanding of the zones and various emotions by their ability to sort the pictures correctly into the zones.

3. Once the students complete the sorting task, instruct them to read the scenario on each page of the book. After each scenario, have the students state which zone it would put them in.
4. Have students choose a corresponding feeling picture from the zone they indicated and attach it with Velcro onto the page to complete the phrase. This provides further assessment opportunities ensuring the students' abilities to use the emotion term in the correct context.

How to adapt this lesson

If students have difficulty reading, read the book aloud. If a student has a short attention span, provide mini-breaks after sorting the pictures and after every few pages.

Figure 4: Example of How Do I Feel Activity

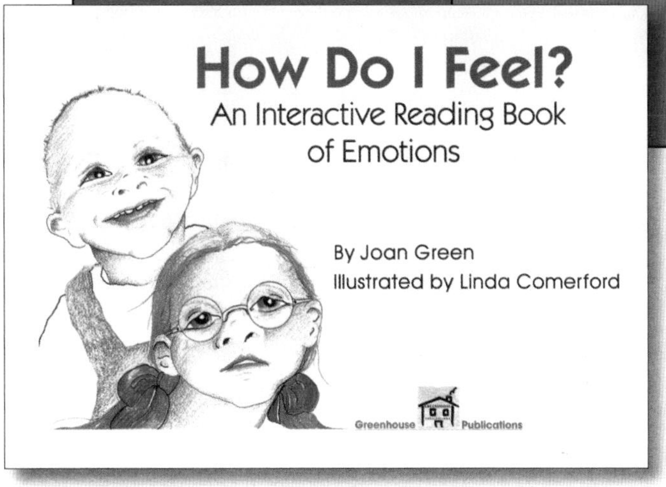

Permission to use visuals of the book *How Do I Feel? An Interactive Reading Book of Emotions* (2006) by Joan Green and illustrated by Linda Comerford was granted by Joan Green. Greenhouse Publications. www.greenhousepub.com

Wrap-up

Ask students to provide more examples of circumstances that change the zone they are in. This will demonstrate how well they can apply what they learned in the activity to meaningful experiences. Restate how quickly people can change zones when events happen. However, if they let others know that they are in the Blue, Yellow, or Red Zone, others may be more understanding. If the students reveal that certain things push them to the Yellow or Red Zone, assure them that you will try to be careful to not do those things and work so they occur less frequently.

Ways to generalize learning

- Inform parents of the learning concept and ask them to help students keep a list of circumstances that influence them to change their zone at home and in the community (this can later be used in Lesson 9: Caution! Triggers Ahead). This can also be done in school.

Additional learning activity for Lesson 7

Zone Idioms (Reproducible M)

Read aloud or make flash cards of idioms and have students guess what emotion and zone those idioms describe. Explain the meaning of the expressions and have students describe a circumstance that made them feel that way. This activity can be turned into a game by dividing groups into teams to guess the idiom's meaning and zone.

ZONE Idioms

Blue Zone

- Down in the dumps
- Downhearted
- Why the long face?
- Feeling blue
- Under the weather

Green Zone

- In seventh heaven
- I feel ten feet tall
- On top of the world
- On cloud nine
- Cool as a cucumber
- Pleased as punch
- I'm cool
- I'm down with that

Yellow Zone

- Wound up
- At my wit's end
- Butterflies in my stomach
- Woke up on the wrong side of the bed
- Chip on your shoulder
- Cause a stir
- At the end of your rope
- Under the wire
- Ants in your pants
- Fish out of water

Red Zone

- Lost my cool
- Ready to boil
- Blow off some steam
- About to explode
- Mad as a hornet
- Beside yourself
- Go bananas
- Go to pieces
- Come apart at the seams
- Thrilled to bits
- Over the moon
- Jumping for joy

Lesson 8:
My Zones Across the Day

Goals for this activity

- Students gain awareness that zones fluctuate throughout the day
- Students increase their understanding of personal triggers that influence their zones
- Students gain awareness that they are more successful in the classroom if they remain in the Green Zone
- Students reflect on whether the zone was expected or unexpected and how it affected others' thoughts

Materials

- ☐ One copy of My Zones Across the Day worksheet (Reproducible N) for each student
- ☐ One copy of Thought Bubbles (Reproducible O) for each six students
- ☐ One set of crayons, colored pencils, or markers in each color of the zones for each student
- ☐ Dry erase markers or chalk in each color of the zones

Overview

In this activity, students graph how their zones change in a day. It is designed to help students understand how this fluctuation affects their entire day. They may be surprised to see how much time they spent in an unexpected zone. This activity becomes more powerful when students reflect on how the zone they were in affected the thoughts and feelings of those around them, which is achieved in this activity by gluing on thought bubbles throughout the graph. This activity allows students to reflect on the success of their day and how this corresponds to the zones they experienced. Students also increase their insight on events that triggered them to change zones, helping them become more cognizant of and brace for these events in the future. This activity works best if completed toward the end of the students' day so they have a larger portion of their day on which to reflect (see Figure 5).

Preparation

- On the board, draw a large-scale version of the My Zones Across the Day worksheet and fill in a daily schedule along the bottom of the graph (e.g., get ready for school, drive to school, morning meeting, reading, math, recess, and so on).
- Copy the My Zones Across the Day worksheet for each student.
- Copy the thought bubbles and cut the bubbles apart.
- Write the schedule on the board:
    1. Lead-in
    2. Write schedule on bottom of graph
    3. Make a dot in the zone you were in for each event during your day
    4. Connect dots to make line graph
    5. Fill in and glue on thought bubbles
    6. Wrap-up

Lead-in

1. Begin by asking the students:
   How often do you think we change the zone we are in within a day?
2. Instruct students that they will be doing an activity to figure out the answer and review the goals of the lesson with them.

Activity

1. Tell students that they will be graphing their zones over the course of the day (if it's early in the day, try using the preceding day). Provide the

instructions in the following steps to students while you demonstrate the instructions using the large replica on the board. When completed, it will resemble Figure 5. (Figure 5 can be printed from the book or CD for students to refer to as well.)

2. Instruct students to fill in the top of the worksheet with their name and date.
3. Instruct each student to color the zone boxes on the left side of the graph with the corresponding color if worksheets weren't printed in color.
4. Brainstorm with students the events during their day. Instruct them to fill in the bottom of the graph with their schedule in sequence of the events they came up with. For example, have the students write out their schedule starting from when they get up in the morning, leave the house, and then each shift in location across the day (e.g., homeroom, math, science, and lunch). See Figure 5 for an example.

Figure 5: Example of a completed My Zones Across the Day worksheet

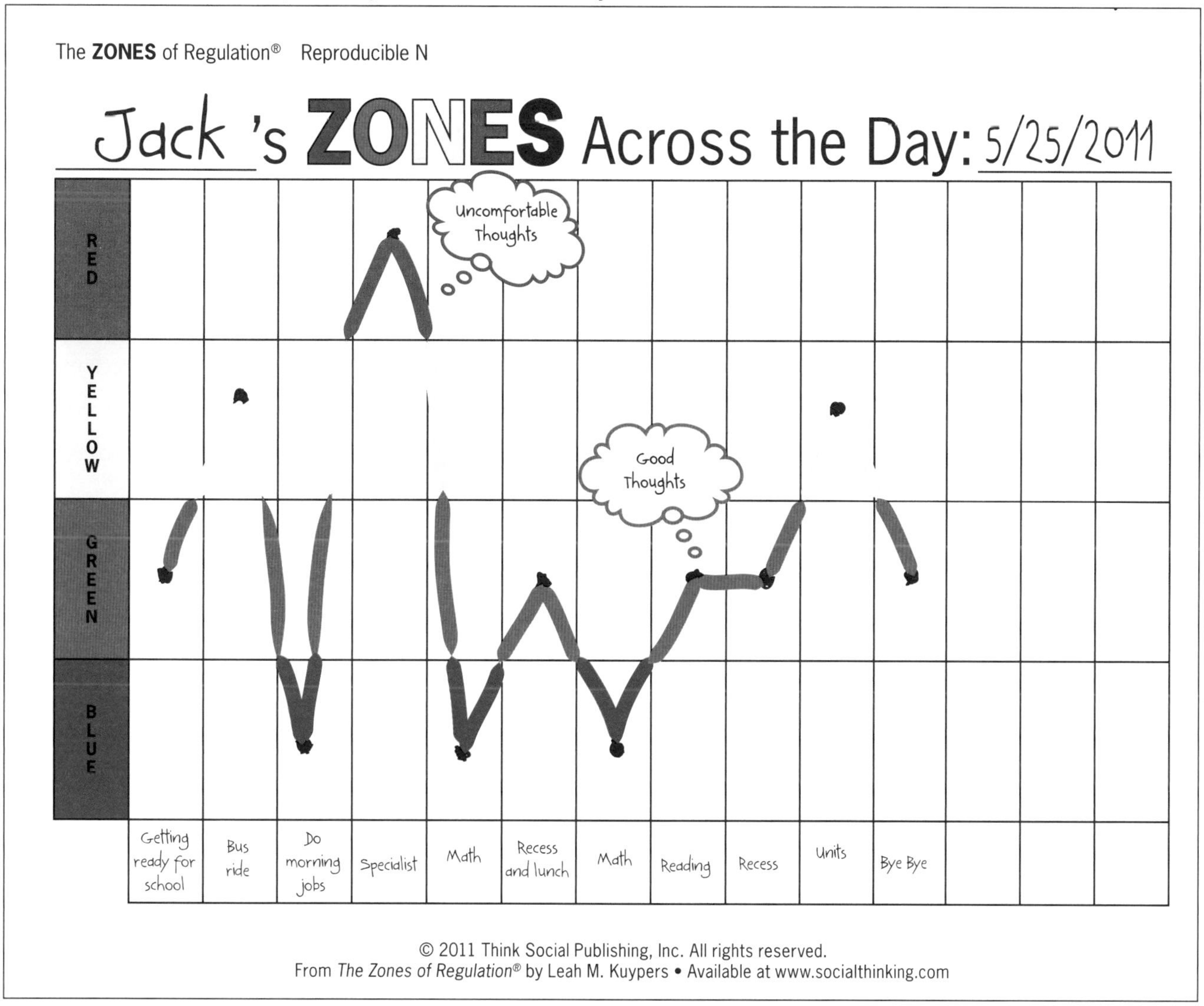

5. Have the students reflect on each event in their day and put a dot on the graph for what zone they were in for that period of time.
6. Use the colored writing utensils to connect the dots to make a line graph. Refer the students to the zone boxes on the left to determine which color to use to draw the line segments. For example, if a student starts out in the Blue Zone and then moves to the Green Zone for the next event, have the student use a blue colored pencil to draw the line through the Blue Zone box, then a green colored pencil that connects from where the blue colored pencil stopped, through the Green Zone box, projecting to where the next event's color will start. See Figure 5 for an example.
7. Discuss with students if their zone was expected or unexpected at each point/period, giving those around them good thoughts or uncomfortable thoughts. Have them fill out and glue on a thought bubble for several points, sharing the kinds of thoughts they suspect others around them were having about them in that zone.

How to adapt this lesson

- If students have difficulty printing, you can fill out their schedule along the bottom of the graph. If they are less familiar with graphing, you may need to provide more instruction.
- If students have a hard time remembering how they felt at different times during their day, prompt them with reminders or use any behavior data collection to aid them.

Wrap-up

Invite students to share their graphed zones with the class and report how many zones they were in over the course of the day. Probe students and assess their ability to reflect on their behavior by asking the students to discuss the following:

What are your thoughts about your day?
Are there any parts you would like to change?
What sort of things or circumstances caused you to change zones?

Explain that it is normal for their zones to fluctuate throughout the day. If they find themselves frequently in the Red Zone, often remain in the Yellow Zone, or spend too much time in the Blue Zone, they need to learn tools that help them get back to and stay in the Green Zone. By using tools that help them change which zone they are in, they are better able to self-regulate. Have each student store the My Zones Across the Day worksheet in their Zones Folder.

Ways to generalize learning

- Send a copy of the worksheet home to families to provide communication about the student's day as well as to help facilitate discussions between students and parents about what is happening at school. Too often when a parent asks a student, "How was your day?," the student will respond, "Fine," and that is the end of the conversation. By graphing one's zones for a day, a parent can encourage the student, "Looks like English went well. Nice job staying in the Green Zone during the exam," as well as work together to problem solve solutions to difficult circumstances, such as "What happened in math that put you in the Yellow Zone?"

- The My Zones Across the Day worksheet (Reproducible N) can be a continuous learning activity that students complete daily to increase awareness of how their zones fluctuate throughout the day (self-regulation). This will help them to see the bigger picture of how this fluctuation can affect their success. The students can self-monitor what zone they are in after every class period or complete this activity at the end of the day. Because this is a self-assessment worksheet, students get immediate feedback on their performance, making it more likely they can become more conscious of when they need to modify their actions.
- My Zones Across the Day can be used instead of a point sheet to have students reflect on their behaviors over the course of a day.

Additional ways to use the Lesson 8 activity

As the students use the lessons in Chapter 4 to learn strategies to aid them in self-regulation, you can use the My Zones Across the Day worksheet to assess if the students are improving their ability to self-regulate. This improvement will be shown by their line graph becoming more linear. This worksheet can be used alongside a point sheet, and the two could be compared at the end of the day to help students see the correlation with points earned and time spent in the Green Zone.

________'s ZONES Across the Day: ________

RED														
YELLOW														
GREEN														
BLUE														

Others were thinking...
Others were thinking...
Others were thinking...
Others were thinking...
Others were thinking...
Others were thinking...
Others were thinking...
Others were thinking...
Others were thinking...
Others were thinking...
Others were thinking...
Others were thinking...
Others were thinking...
Others were thinking...
Others were thinking...
Others were thinking...
Others were thinking...
Others were thinking...
Others were thinking...
Others were thinking...
Others were thinking...
Others were thinking...
Others were thinking...
Others were thinking...

Lesson 9:
Caution! Triggers Ahead

Goals for this activity

- Students gain awareness that they are more successful if they can stay in the Green Zone
- Students recognize their personal triggers that lead to the Red or Yellow Zone
- Students work on problem solving to avoid triggers

Materials

- ☐ One sheet of yellow construction paper or one Triggers worksheet (Reproducible P) for each student
- ☐ Yellow marker, crayon, or colored pencil if using worksheet
- ☐ Black marker if using construction paper
- ☐ Writing utensils

Overview

In this activity, students reflect on what events or "triggers" push them into the Yellow and Red Zones. To do this, they brainstorm with a partner their triggers and complete an individualized worksheet. When students are able to identify their triggers, they become more cognizant of their state of alertness and are better able to brace themselves for what is to come. This allows them more time to apply problem solving strategies or utilize tools to cope.

Note to teacher: When students can identify their triggers, adults who work closely with the students then have a responsibility to help the students regulate around triggers. This includes preparing students before a trigger occurs, such as giving notice that there will be a fire drill if a student reports that loud noises are a trigger. This also includes removing triggers when possible; for example, a teacher can stop wearing perfume if a student is sensitive to smells or can differentiate a math assignment as an accommodation if a student reports it is too hard.

Preparation

- Complete a sample Triggers worksheet for students to reference of your triggers
- Copy a Triggers worksheet for each student. Alternatively, cut yellow construction paper into a square for each student, and then turn it to make a diamond and write "CAUTION: Triggers Ahead" across the middle in black marker.
- Write the schedule on the board:
  1. Lead-in
  2. Think of your triggers
  3. Pair up with partner to discuss triggers
  4. Share triggers with class
  5. Fill in Caution sign with triggers
  6. Wrap-up

Lead-in

1. Hook the students by telling them a personal story about yourself and one of your triggers; for example:

   I am in the Yellow Zone when I feel like I have too much to do and not enough time to do it. I know that I need to proceed with caution when this happens so I don't end up in the Red Zone. I sometimes have a deadline or something I need to get done, but I don't feel like I can possibly do it all without going crazy. This makes me very stressed and anxious, and often I become crabbier when I am overwhelmed. It doesn't take much to push me into the Red Zone when I feel this way.

2. Review that these events are called triggers, and we need to be aware of them so we can take CAUTION! Review with students that when they see a CAUTION sign, they know that they need to prepare themselves for something out of the ordinary and to be more careful. They often see signs such as "CAUTION! Road Construction Ahead" or "CAUTION! Slippery When Wet" warning them of danger. Tell students that they will be thinking about their triggers that lead them to the Yellow or Red Zone.
3. Share the activities and goals of the lesson.

Figure 6:
Example of Triggers worksheet

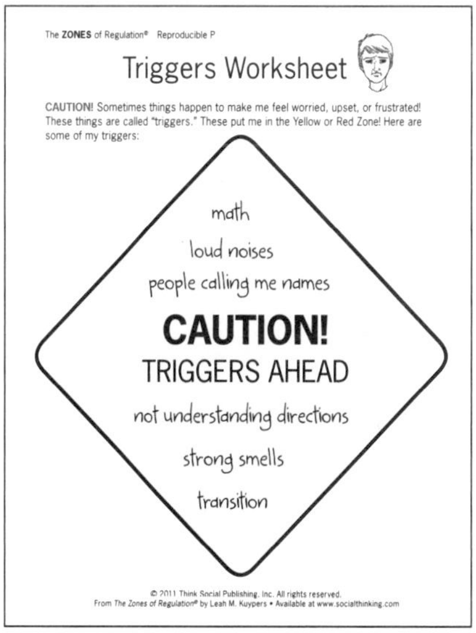

Activity

1. Describe to students how to make their own CAUTION sign (as in Figure 6) and fill it in with their triggers (provide a visual example for their reference).
2. Ask students to think about triggers they experience in their own lives. Ask them to reflect on the last week and the events that pushed them into the Red and Yellow Zones.
3. Have students write down any triggers they think of on the worksheet. If they're using the worksheet, ask students to color their CAUTION sign yellow.
4. Have students pair up with a partner and share their triggers with each other. Encourage students to add to their list of triggers and to help each other identify their triggers.
5. Come back together as a large group and have students take turns sharing their triggers with the whole group.
6. Students can continue to add to their personal lists throughout the activity as well as in the future as they encounter less regulating events.
7. Assess the students' insights into recognizing their triggers by their participation in the discussion and by observation of their completed Triggers worksheets. Some triggers the students identify will require additional analysis with the student to get down to the root of the problem. If a student lists math, for example, ask what it is about math that he or she dislikes (is it too hard, the writing involved, etc.). Some identified triggers may require you to alter your behavior or approach with students or make accommodations to avoid triggers.

Wrap-up

To continue to assess for understanding through discussion, ask students the following:

Why do you think it is important to recognize your own triggers?
How will this help you?

Note to Teacher

Identifying triggers is often difficult for many students who struggle with regulation, so it may be helpful to receive some insight from family members or other teachers or staff if you are less familiar with the events that cause the students to lose some control.

Younger students may benefit from visual expression of their triggers instead of written ones. If students are not able to identify triggers, you will need to directly teach students what events push them into the Yellow or Red Zone and need to be avoided or problem solved.

How is it helpful to know each other's triggers?
What will you do differently if you know what triggers your peers?
How could this influence the class as a whole?
What will you do the next time you detect one of your triggers?

Discuss with students that when they are able to recognize what pushes them into the Yellow or Red Zone, they can do something about it. Explain that, as their teacher, you can help them better if you understand what causes them to go into the Yellow or Red Zone. More importantly, the students can help themselves if they understand what is getting in their way of success. Provide an example of how you could help a student, how a student could help a peer, and how someone could help oneself if aware of triggers. Have each student store his or her Triggers worksheet in the Zones Folder.

Ways to generalize learning

- Send a copy home of the completed Triggers worksheet for students' families, encouraging parents to add to the list of triggers with the student.
- To encourage students to think and increase their awareness about others, have students create a Triggers worksheet for people in their family or people with whom they work closely, such as teachers or aides. Probe them to consider what the triggers are that lead people close to them into the Yellow or Red Zone, reflecting on any of their behaviors that could serve as triggers to those close to them.
- The Triggers worksheet can be helpful for entire families to complete together as a means to assist everyone to become more aware of what is interfering with each member staying in the Green Zone and to create a more supportive and nurturing environment. You may also want to do this with your work colleagues.

Triggers Worksheet

CAUTION! Sometimes things happen to make me feel worried, upset, or frustrated! These things are called "triggers." These put me in the Yellow or Red Zone! Here are some of my triggers:

Ways to Check for Learning

The following informal assessment techniques are provided as ways you can gauge students' understanding of The Zones. It is up to you to determine how to conduct the informal assessments and which ones will be most helpful with your students.

Check-In

This activity was designed to informally assess a student's ability to recognize how he or she is feeling using the concept of the zones on an ongoing basis. Once students are taught the concept of the zones in Lesson 1, you can use the Check-In activity to pick up where you left off in the last lesson and to observe how students are learning the information. You should do this at the beginning of each lesson (or more frequently, such as at the beginning of each subject/class) once Lesson 1 is completed. There are several ways the Check-In may be conducted given the students' needs, examples of which are given below:

- Use the Zones Check-In. (Figure 7; see the instructions in "Visual Supports for ways to check for learning," later in this chapter).
- Write on the board: *I feel* ________. *I'm in the* ________ *Zone,* and have students report orally.

  Attach a Zones Flip Book to students' desks for easy manipulation and cueing (Figure 8; see the instructions in "Visual supports for ways to check for learning"). Ask the students to flip to their zone at the beginning of each subject and continue to do so as often as the students feel they change zones.
- Use the Wall Posters of The Zones that are displayed in the classroom (Figure 9; see Lesson 1 for instructions) and have photos or names of each student to place on or next to the large visual of the zones. You can use Velcro® to attach photographs or cards with the student's name on it, or use clothespins with the student's name written on them.
- Students report orally.

Observing student behavior

You can also informally assess students by observing their behavior. The following are examples of opportunities for such observation:

- Students spontaneously describe how they are feeling using the zones. This can be measured through random conversation, students independently manipulating their pictures on The Zones Wall Posters, or flipping to a different zone in their Zone Flip Books.
- When students indicate their zone, use the response and your subjective opinion to measure their ability to correctly recognize their zone. If you disagree with the students' responses, gently point out why you see them differently. This may be done by describing how the student is looking (e.g., "Are you sure you are in the Blue Zone? I see you smiling and sitting up straight.") or acting (e.g., "You are having a difficult

time staying in your seat and demonstrating whole body listening. Is there a better zone to describe how you are feeling?").

Visual supports for ways to check for learning

(included on the CD)

The informal assessment Check-In activity uses visuals. Described here are directions for preparing these visual supports:

- Zones Check-In
- Zones Flip Book
- Wall Posters of The Zones

You will need to prepare these visuals before you begin the activity with students. As discussed earlier, you can customize which activities and visual supports you use, depending on students' ages and grade levels, verbal abilities, cognition, and the size of the group.

Zones Check-In (Figure 7) (see Reproducible Q below):

For older students

1. Print the Zones Check-In template.
2. Laminate the Zones Check-In template.

This can be used as a whiteboard on which students use dry erase markers to write in their answers or as a visual reference for students to orally report their feelings and zones.

For younger students (or nonverbal students): Making a modified communication board

When using the Zones Check-In with younger or nonverbal students, modify it so that it becomes a communication board to help facilitate the check-in process (see Figure 7 and Reproducible Q).

1. Print the Zones Check-In template with the icons of the four zones (Reproducible Q), and emotions pictures (Reproducible C).
2. Laminate the Zones Check-In template.
3. Color in the four icons of the zones with their respective colors if printed in black and white. If additional cuing is necessary for the students, outline the edge of the emotion picture with the corresponding color zone.
4. Laminate the four zone icons and emotions pictures.
5. Cut apart the four icons of the zones and emotion pictures.
6. Adhere small pieces (½" x ½") Velcro® to the middle of the backs of the icons representing the zones as well as the emotion pictures. When working with a preschool or population with cognitive challenges, it's recommended you start with the basic emotions, such as sad, tired, happy, calm, silly, and mad before adding more complex ones. Make sure you have at least one emotion representing each color of the zones.

7. Place a small piece of the opposite side of the Velcro to the Zones Check-In modified communication board in the middle of the two small boxes (e.g., "I feel □." and "I am in the □ Zone."). Place two or three strips of Velcro (depending on how many emotions you are using) across the width of the page below the sentence "I am in the □ Zone." Adhere all the emotion pictures to the first one or two strips of Velcro and the Zone icons to the bottom strip. See Figure 7 for an example.

To use this to check in, present the communication board to one student at a time. Read the first sentence to the student and instruct him or her to choose the emotion picture that best describes how he or she is feeling. Then read the second sentence and allow the student to choose which zone matches the emotion.

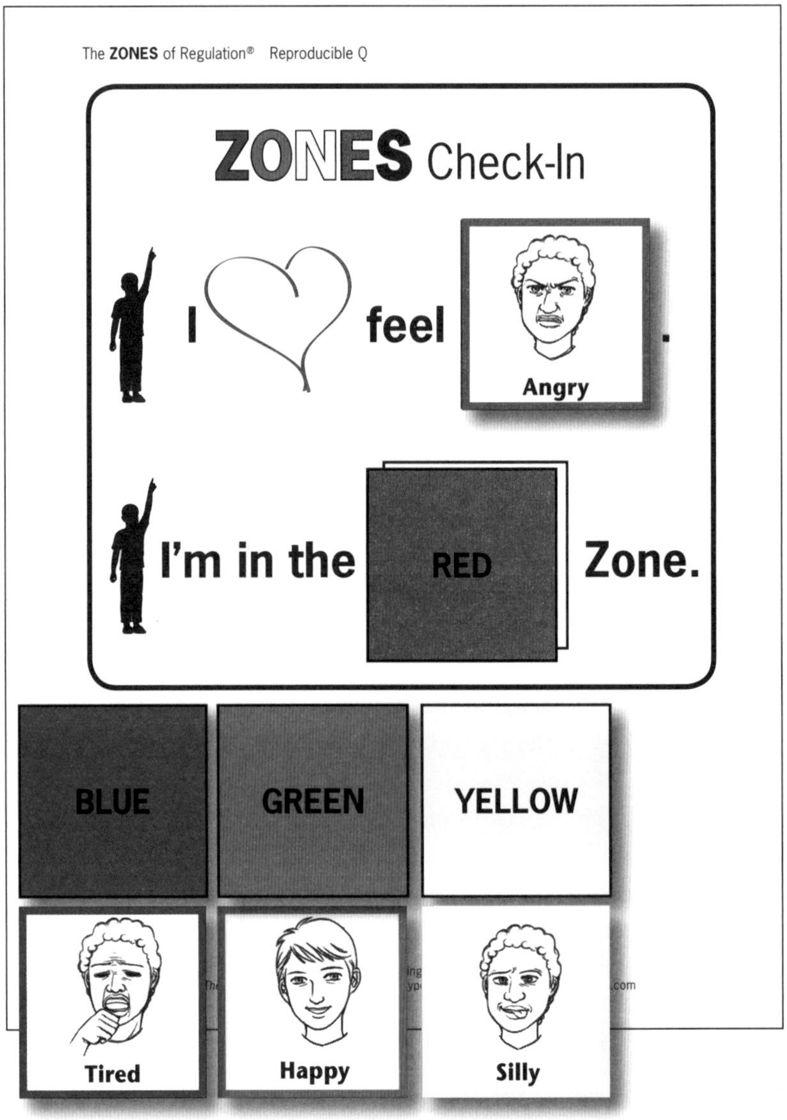

Figure 7:
Example of Zones Check-In modified into a communication board (for younger and nonverbal students).

ZONES Check-In

 I  feel ______ .

 I'm in the ______ Zone.

Icons of the Four ZONES

Cut out the visuals below if modifying Zones Check-In into a communication board.

BLUE	**GREEN**
YELLOW	**RED**

Zones Flip Book

Instructions are provided below to assemble a Zones Flip Book using colored construction paper.

1. Cut out two rectangles (about the size of a 3" x 5"note card) in each of the four colors (blue, green, yellow, and red). Also cut out two white rectangles so you have a total of ten rectangles that are all the same size.
2. Glue the white to the blue, then blue to green, green to yellow, yellow to red, then the red to the white rectangle. You will have five sets of rectangular cards.
3. Laminate each of the five sets of cards for added durability.
4. Arrange the cards so the top and bottom of the Flip Book will be white. Stack the five cards together so that the two blue sides, two green sides, two yellow sides, and two red sides face each other. As you flip through the book, you will see the same color on the top page as on the bottom page as seen in Figure 8.
5. Packing tape, a spiral binder, or rings can be used to make the cards into a book.
6. Tape the white bottom of the book to the student's desk, so the student can flip the book open to the zone he or she is in (the zone color will be open on the top of the desk, as well as hanging down so the teacher can see the student's zone).
7. You may choose to personalize each student's flip book with emotion pictures that represent how they often feel in each zone and/or put in pictures of the tools they can use while in that zone.

Figure 8.
Example of Zones Flip Book

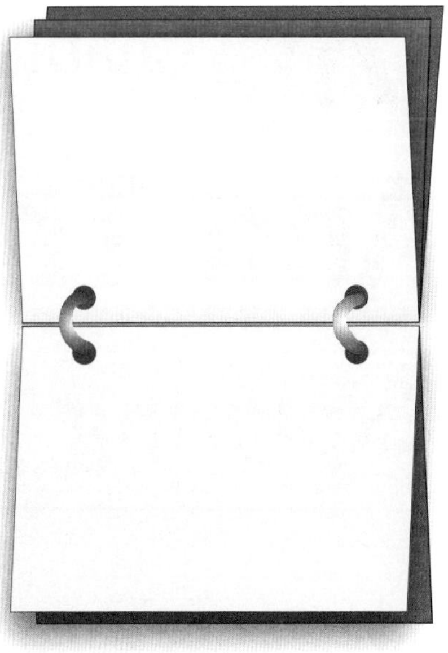

Wall Posters of The Zones

The directions to make this visual support are explained in Lesson 1. It is an activity that can be done with the students as part of their learning.

Figure 9:
Example of Wall Posters of The Zones with student names

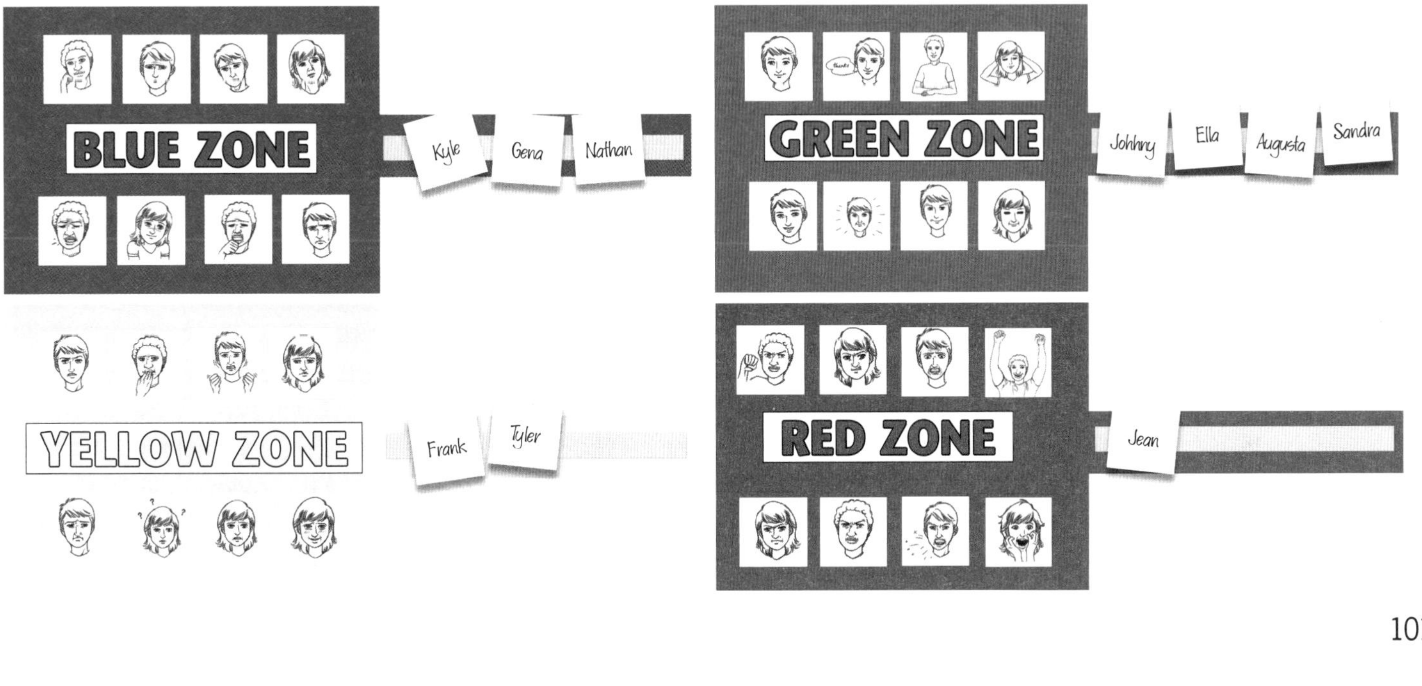

Chapter 4

And They're Off

Exploring Tools to Calm and Alert

In the lessons presented in this chapter, students learn and practice tools that can help them regulate their zones. (The lessons in Chapter 5 focus on understanding when to use these tools.) As discussed earlier, you are encouraged to do these lessons gradually throughout the teaching of The Zones curriculum. They also can be done in any order. Each lesson provides background information about the types of tools being offered to students and tips for their presentation.

Goals for this chapter

By the end of the chapter, students will be learning to:

- Understand that there are strategies or tools they can use that will influence their zones (Lessons 10, 11, and 12)
- Understand that tools affect each person differently and they need to determine which tools are most effective for them (Lessons 10, 11, and 12)
- Know at least five strategies they find calming, at least two strategies they find alerting, and at least one strategy that helps them remain in the Green Zone (Lessons 10, 11, and 12)
- Be able to demonstrate the use of a strategy to self-regulate (Lessons 10, 11, and 12)

In the lessons in this chapter, students consider the following essential questions:

- How does the use of a zones tool change the way I think and feel?
- Do all tools affect me in the same way or are some more effective for me than others?

The lessons in this chapter are designed to help students explore a variety of tools and understand how each tool benefits them. It's beneficial to explore a variety of tools as some students gravitate to different types of tools. To help you think about the different types of tools, they are organized into the following categories: sensory supports, calming techniques, and thinking strategies. There is overlap among these categories. Many of the calming techniques combine a component aimed at shifting the physiological reaction the body is having to a stressful situation to calm the nervous system as well as a neuro-cognitive component aimed at changing the brain's pattern of thinking. For example, deep breathing addresses the physiological changes your body experiences as a result of stress and helps to shift your nervous system to a more relaxed state. Deep breathing also addresses a neurological or cognitive component; it helps refocus the brain when you breathe in a sequence or notice your breath's movement by placing your hands on your stomach. It also concurrently helps to get more oxygen to the brain so it can function more effectively.

In addition to addressing the students' sensory needs and teaching calming techniques, it is valuable to teach students about how their thinking patterns can cause them to become less regulated. As discussed earlier, executive functions often lag in students who struggle with self-regulation and are closely tied with the ability to regulate our emotions. Students who struggle with self-regulation frequently tend to be inflexible, black-and-white thinkers, unable to see the shades of gray. They have difficulty with objectivity and seeing the big picture, getting caught up in insignificant details, making it difficult for them to think rationally about their thoughts and feelings. Their self-talk is frequently riddled with self-defeating statements, such as "I can't do this," "I never get to go first," or "No one ever listens to me." Tools that address thinking patterns can be called "thinking strategies," as these work to change one's cognitive thoughts. Numerous curriculum materials and approaches are available to address regulation of thinking patterns as well as anxiety and other emotions, sensory needs, and social skills. For information about some of these publications, see "Recommended Resources" in the Appendix.

This chapter presents three types of tools to help students regulate:

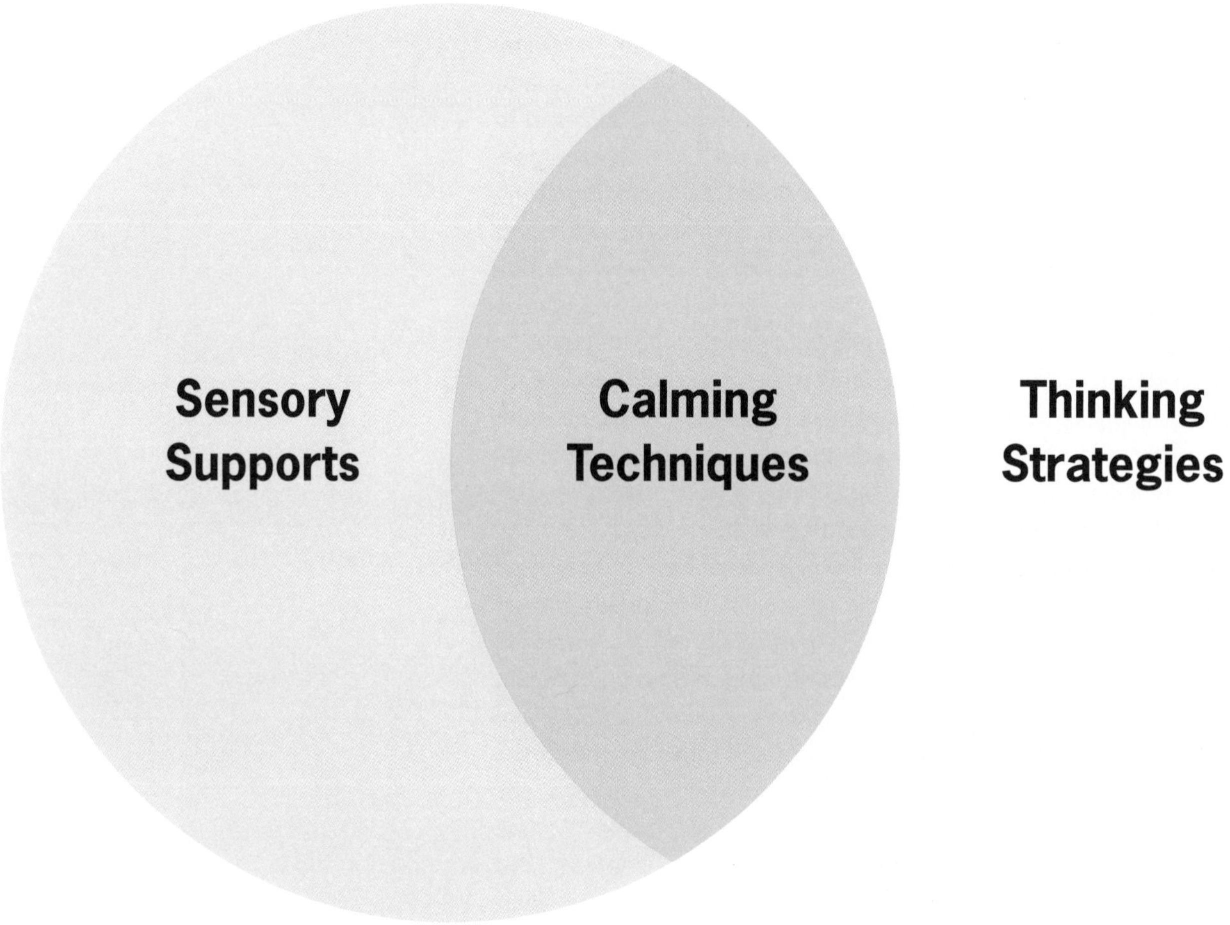

Tools Taught in This Chapter's Lessons

Sensory Supports

- These will depend on the sensory supports and equipment you have available.

Calming Techniques

- 6 Sides of Breathing
- Lazy 8 Breathing
- Calming Sequence
- Count to Ten
- Learning to Take a Deep Breath

Thinking Strategies

- Big vs. Little Problem
- Inner Coach vs. Inner Critic
- Superflex® vs. Rock Brain Thinking

Using the lessons in this chapter

In these lessons, students use the Zones Tools worksheet (Reproducible R) to organize and assess the effectiveness of different tools. If students are learning these tools throughout the teaching of the curriculum, when students get to the point of understanding the zones in themselves (in the lessons in Chapter 3), they will already be aware of some tools they can use to help regulate.

For students to become successful in using tools to regulate, it's best to create continual opportunities for them to practice and gain more comfort in using their tools while they are in the Green Zone. This is especially important for tools a student indicates would help in the Yellow or Red Zone. A student won't attempt a new tool that he or she just tried once when in a heightened state. Rather, that tool needs to be practiced repeatedly while the student is calm, so that when he or she is in the Yellow or Red Zone, it will be routine and natural for that student to use the tool.

It's recommended that the practice time be incorporated into the students' routine so that it happens at a set time every day (for example, after recess or before bed at night). Practicing tools together as a class also helps to create the culture of The Zones, in which everyone is using tools to help themselves feel calm and focused and is speaking the same language. This helps to not single out any student who may struggle with regulation more than others.

In the lessons in this chapter, students explore tools to gauge how each tool affects them. Subsequent lessons are designed to help the students organize their tools into the Zones Toolbox so they have a visual to refer to and a better understanding of when to use their tools. Even when a tool is entered on the Zones Tools worksheet once, add it again and have the student rate the experience a second time. Often when trying a tool for the first time, students are silly or overly concerned about what their peers are experiencing to accurately reflect on their own experience. Students also may have adopted the mantra "nothing works" in dealing with their frustrations or anxieties. Often these students have not practiced the tools in a calm state, but have been told for years to "take a deep breath" or "count to ten" when their coping capacity has already been stripped, leading them to fail at using the tool. You can tell these students, "Nothing ever works the first time, and maybe not the second or third time so we need to practice and practice to get better at something."

Some students are perpetually in the Yellow Zone. They seem to oscillate between silly, anxious, and frustrated but rarely appear to be in the Green Zone for any duration of time. It is important to take time with these students so they gain a better understanding of what their Green Zone feels like. In addition to the tools explored in these lessons, students may benefit from guided imagery (numerous resources are available for download from the iTunes Store and www.amazon.com), mental visualization (e.g., picture yourself in your favorite place, draw a picture of the place, tell me about it, create a book full of pictures that are calming for the student, as in "Additional learning activity for Lesson 11"), Brain Gym®, or yoga.

Lesson Plans and Learning Activities

Lesson 10:
Exploring Sensory Support Tools

Overview

In this activity, students rotate through stations that have a variety of sensory tools to explore sensory supports and discover how the various sensory supports affect their level of alertness. The specific sensory tools used will vary depending on the materials and tools you have available for use by students. See "Materials" in this lesson for suggestions.

Goals for this activity

- Students gain insight about how sensory support tools can help regulate zones
- Students understand that sensory support tools can help them wake up and be more alert as well as help them calm down and feel more organized
- Students understand that sensory support tools should be used in all zones in order to self-regulate
- Students learn how to access and use sensory support tools

Materials

The specific materials you present to students in this lesson depend on the sensory supports and equipment to which you have access. Listed below are several recommended sensory supports to try. Some require specialized equipment, such as a swing, that you may not have available for student use. If this is the case, students can explore many other recommended sensory supports using objects commonly found in a school or home, such as carrying a stack of heavy books.

Two of the websites from which you can order sensory items are www.abilitations.com and www.southpawenterpises.com.

Background information

Everyone has sensations they seek out as well as ones they avoid. For example, you might enjoy smelling perfumes or find incense calming. Others might find these same smells or stimuli noxious, and this in turn causes them to feel less regulated and uncomfortable. Sensory tools, such as those listed with this lesson, can be used to help calm or alert the central nervous system, so students are better able to attend to and focus on relevant stimuli and filter out irrelevant, background stimuli. By providing students with the sensory input they crave in a meaningful, adaptive way, students' central nervous systems will become more organized, and students will be less likely to engage in disruptive behaviors to get their sensory needs met.

Some students find it effective to use sensory supports at their seats that help meet their need to touch things (such as playing with a fidget ball), move (such as sit on a therapy ball rather than a chair), and work their muscles (such as tying a stretch band or fabric around the legs of a desk so the student can pull and push against it with his or her legs). Other students require more intense activities, such as heavy work, running, climbing, crashing, swinging, and burrowing under pillows/bean bags, to help them reach an optimal state of alertness for learning and socializing.

Students who have sensory processing difficulties require an individualized "sensory diet" of tailored activities that help organize their sensory system for improved modulation and regulation. Sensory tools listed in this lesson are by no means comprehensive. Students will find some sensory tools more powerful for regulation than others, and it is intended that the list of tools used be customized for individual students. For more information on sensory integration and processing, consult with a skilled occupational therapist with training in the area of sensory processing disorder and refer to the books *Sensational Kids: Hope and Help for Children with Sensory Processing Disorder* and *The Out-of-Sync Child: Recognizing and Coping with Sensory Processing Disorder.* The Alert Program® is valuable to help students further learn about and explore sensory supports (see "Recommended Resources" for more information).

Note to teacher: Although occupational therapists have extensive background in sensory integration theory, many classroom teachers and parents are skilled at carrying out the everyday sensory supports with students. This activity can be done within a classroom facilitated by the teacher or in the home facilitated by a parent who has working knowledge and experience in helping with students with sensory needs. If sensory processing disorders are new to you, it is recommended that you co-teach this lesson with an occupational therapist or that it be taught by an occupational therapist. If a student is experiencing significant sensory seeking or defensive behaviors, it is highly recommended that you consult with an occupational therapist trained in working with students with Sensory Processing Disorder. Sensory seeking can be defined as needing to experience a sense at a far greater intensity than what would be typically expected for a child of that age. It is often seen as the student seeking movement, touch, and/or input to the muscles and joints (such as through crashing, squeezing, jumping, bumping, and rolling). Sensory defensiveness can be described as experiencing a sensation that is tolerable to most as extremely unpleasant. This is often seen with the sense of touch (e.g., sensitive to different clothing textures or a dislike for grooming activities), hearing (sensitive to sounds), taste (e.g., being a picky eater), smell (more sensitive to odors than others), and movement (e.g., unsure of footing on unstable surfaces).

Preparation

- Copy one Zones Tools Worksheet for each student.
- Set up stations for using the different supports at different locations around the room. Determine the amount of time each student will spend at a particular station. This will depend on the time available for the learning activity and the number of students. Make sure to allow enough time for the students to record what tool they are using, determine the zone(s) in which it would be beneficial, and transition between stations. Students can record more than one zone per tool.
- Make a list of all of the sensory supports on the board for students to refer to for spelling.
- Write the schedule on the board:
  1. Lead-in
  2. Rotate through stations, record zone
  3. Wrap-up

Lead-in

1. Instruct the students that they will be rotating through stations to explore different sensory support tools and rate their effect.
2. Share the activities and goals of the lesson.

Materials (continued)

- ☐ Sensory tools to explore, such as any of the following:
  - Squeezing a fidget ball or Silly Putty®/theraputty
  - Digging in or hunting for objects in a rice bin
  - Sitting with a weighted blanket, vest, or lap pad
  - Sitting on a Move-n-sit or Disc-o-sit cushion (both examples of inflatable cushions that provide a student seated on it with a subtle movement experience)
  - Wearing noise-canceling headphones
  - Wall push-ups
  - Pushing, pulling, or carrying something heavy (meaningful activities that involve heavy work, such as stacking chairs, pushing a cart, carrying a loaded basket/stack of books, pushing a broom or mop, or wiping down tables or blackboards)
  - Swinging (on the playground swings or monkey bars or on an indoor suspended swing if available)
  - Playing on scooter boards
  - Jumping (with a jump rope or on a trampoline)
  - Riding a bike or scooter
  - Deep pressure squishes with a bean bag or an oversized pillow
  - Bouncing on a therapy ball
  - Burrowing in pillows/cushions/blankets
- ☐ One Zones Tools worksheet (Reproducible R) for each student
- ☐ Colored pencils in colors of zones
- ☐ A timer

WEIGH STATION

Potential Blue Zone/ Alerting Tools

Blue Zone ideas to explore with students include the following: chewing gum, eating tart candy, drinking water, doodling, exercising, completing Brain Gym® moves, listening to lively music, and getting fresh air.

Activity

1. Start students at different stations or desks with a sensory support tool. Invite them to utilize this first sensory tool while you review the goals and directions of the lesson.
2. Explain that they will rotate stations throughout the activity so they get a chance to experience all of the sensory tools. While using the tool at each station, they need to consider if the tool helped them feel calmer, more awake, or if it had no effect. If they notice it was calming or alerting, have them make the connection that they need a calming tool in the Yellow and Red Zones and an alerting tool in the Blue Zone.
3. Have students use the worksheet to circle the zone(s) in which they feel the tool would be helpful (see Figure 10). Inform students that it is acceptable to circle more than one zone for each tool or indicate that it would help in "none" of the Zones.
   Note to teacher: The Zones Tools worksheet will vary for each student, as each student sees what tools are effective for himself or herself. Do not try to push students to circle a particular zone on the worksheet, but point out what you noticed while they participated with the tool.
4. After students have completed the worksheet for that tool, have students rotate stations.
5. As students rotate through the stations, walk around and assess if the students' judgments of which tools would help in each zone are consistent with your observations.
6. As students participate in the different stations, provide further explanation of how tools can assist in regulating their emotions and bodies. Tailor the language depending on the grade level of the students. Instruct the students that some sensory support tools help them wake up and feel more alert if they are in the Blue Zone, some help them calm down and focus if they are in the Yellow or Red Zone, and some help them stay in the Green Zone. Today they get to test out different sensory tools to see what they think will be the most helpful.
   - Ask students what their day would look like if they stayed in the Blue Zone all day and what would be the consequences of this. Explain the importance of having tools and strategies they can use to wake them up.
   - Ask students what their day would look like if they stayed in the Yellow Zone all day and what would be the consequences of this. Explain the importance of having tools and strategies they can use to slow them down.

Wrap-up

Facilitate a group discussion, inviting the students to share tools they found helped to calm them down, wake them up, and help keep them in the Green Zone. Discuss that everyone is different and what works for one student will be different from what works for another. Have students save their Zones Tools worksheet in their Zones Folders.

Ways to generalize learning

As discussed earlier, it is imperative to set aside time daily for students to practice the tools. If a student is experiencing sensory differences, it is vital that he or she is able to access the sensory supports proactively so the student has a meaningful and adaptive way of getting his or her sensory needs met. If the student's sensory needs aren't being accommodated, the student will still find a way to meet his or her sensory needs, but in a more disruptive and maladaptive manner (for example, getting out of his or her seat unexpectedly, rolling around during circle time, running when walking is the expectation, or bumping/touching others).

As sensory supports are explored using the Zones Tools worksheet and it becomes apparent what is most effective for the student, it is imperative that all staff are brought on board to support the student in accessing his or her tools to get the sensory needs met. Sharing the Zones Toolbox that the student creates in the next chapter will assist in this process.

The **ZONES** of Regulation® Reproducible R   Name: Jane Doe

ZONES Tools Worksheet

Name of Tool	Circle the zone or zones you think the tool would help in.				
rice bin	Blue	Green	Yellow	Red	None
putty	Blue	Green	Yellow	Red	None
cushion	Blue	Green	Yellow	Red	None
fidget ball	Blue	Green	Yellow	Red	None
headphones	Blue	Green	Yellow	Red	None
sit on ball	Blue	Green	Yellow	Red	None
weighted vest	Blue	Green	Yellow	Red	None
rub back	Blue	Green	Yellow	Red	None
	Blue	Green	Yellow	Red	None
	Blue	Green	Yellow	Red	None
	Blue	Green	Yellow	Red	None
	Blue	Green	Yellow	Red	None
	Blue	Green	Yellow	Red	None
	Blue	Green	Yellow	Red	None
	Blue	Green	Yellow	Red	None
	Blue	Green	Yellow	Red	None
	Blue	Green	Yellow	Red	None
	Blue	Green	Yellow	Red	None
	Blue	Green	Yellow	Red	None
	Blue	Green	Yellow	Red	None

Figure 10:
Example of Zones Tools worksheet

 Name: ______________________

ZONES Tools Worksheet

Name of Tool	Circle the zone or zones you think the tool would help in.				
	Blue	Green	Yellow	Red	None
	Blue	Green	Yellow	Red	None
	Blue	Green	Yellow	Red	None
	Blue	Green	Yellow	Red	None
	Blue	Green	Yellow	Red	None
	Blue	Green	Yellow	Red	None
	Blue	Green	Yellow	Red	None
	Blue	Green	Yellow	Red	None
	Blue	Green	Yellow	Red	None
	Blue	Green	Yellow	Red	None
	Blue	Green	Yellow	Red	None
	Blue	Green	Yellow	Red	None
	Blue	Green	Yellow	Red	None
	Blue	Green	Yellow	Red	None
	Blue	Green	Yellow	Red	None
	Blue	Green	Yellow	Red	None
	Blue	Green	Yellow	Red	None
	Blue	Green	Yellow	Red	None
	Blue	Green	Yellow	Red	None
	Blue	Green	Yellow	Red	None

Lesson 11:
Exploring Tools for Calming

Goals for this activity

- Students learn about and try out calming techniques that can be utilized to calm their body and mind
- Students gain insight into how calming techniques help regulate zones
- Students reflect on which tools are effective in regulating themselves

Materials

- ☐ One Zones Tools worksheet (Reproducible R) for each student. If one was started for sensory support tools, continue to use that same one.
- ☐ The Six Sides of Breathing visual (Reproducible S)
- ☐ Lazy 8 Breathing visual (Reproducible T)
- ☐ My Calming Sequence visual (Reproducible U)
- ☐ One blank piece of paper for each student
- ☐ Colored pencils in colors of the zones

Overview

In this activity, students practice several calming techniques together and reflect on the techniques using the Zones Tools worksheet. The calming techniques used are:

- Learning to Take a Deep Breath
- Six Sides of Breathing (a breathing technique that uses a hexagon to structure breaths)
- Lazy 8 Breathing (a breathing technique that uses a lazy eight to structure breaths)
- Count to Ten
- Calming Sequence (a meditative routine to follow that repeats steps consisting of muscle contraction and deep pressure input)

These calming techniques incorporate both a physiological component that helps to calm the sensory and nervous system as well as a cognitive component to calm the mind. Often these tools can help students to regulate their emotions—to help get them out of the autonomic "fight, freight, or flight" state that the body goes into when reacting to intense situations.

Preparation

- Copy visuals of calming techniques that will be introduced (Reproducibles S, T, and U).
- Make one copy of the Zones Tools worksheet (Reproducible R) for each student if the students don't already have one. (If students completed Lesson 10, they can continue to use the same worksheet.)
- Make a list of the calming tools they will explore on the board that the students can refer to for spelling if they aren't spelled out in the schedule.
- Practice how to do and teach these techniques by reading the description in the Activity steps and consulting the visuals included with this lesson. **Note to teacher:** Several of the techniques used in this activity incorporate deep breathing, yet many students have a difficult time coordinating the rhythm of deep breathing. Often a student may appear to be hyperventilating rather than relaxing when you first attempt deep breathing exercises. If, while introducing the calming techniques below, you identify students struggling with the coordination of deep breathing, set aside some time to address this skill before continuing to move on through the lesson. Play some relaxing music, dim the lights, and have students lie down on the floor and place their hands over their stomachs. Ask them to pretend they have a balloon in their stomach

that they slowly blow up so they can feel it expand with their hands. Then, instruct them to slowly let out the air (without making any sound effects). You can also try placing a book or object on their stomachs so they can watch it rise and fall with their breath. The goal is for students to use their diaphragm to help them take deep breaths, which helps to reduce muscle tension and get more oxygen into their bloodstream. Challenge students to see who can take the slowest deep breath. If it's needed and would be all right with the students and school policy, you might try placing your hands on their lower rib cage to help facilitate the breathing through light manual manipulation. Often students laugh, giggle, or act out the first time deep breathing is introduced as is often the case when they are uncomfortable with learning any new skill. Set aside a time every day to work with students on learning how to take deep breaths when they are in calm states, and soon the laughter will subside.

- Write the schedule on the board:
  1. Lead-in
  2. Practice calming tools
     - Six Sides of Breathing
     - Lazy 8 Breathing
     - Calming Sequence
     - Count to Ten
  3. Record tools
  4. Wrap-up

Lead-in

1. Introduce to the students that they will be learning about calming techniques that often help relax people's minds and bodies. Invite students to share any strategies they currently use to calm down that would work in the Red or Yellow Zone:

   We've talked about how it is often unexpected to be in the Red and Yellow Zones. Now we need to figure out some tools or strategies we can use to help us get back to the Green Zone. Do any of you have a strategy that you use to help you calm down?

2. Inform them they will learn new tools to add to their existing ones and review the goal of the lesson with students. Review how it feels to be calm, highlighting the physiological feel of the body and brain. Refer them to their Me in the Green Zone (Lesson 5) self-portrait in their Zones Folder for cues.

   How do you know that you are calm? What do you look like? How does your body feel? How do others think about you when you are calm?

Activity

1. Explain to students they will be working on exploring zone tools that may help them to calm down when they are in the Yellow or Red Zone.
2. Give each student a "The Six Sides of Breathing" handout. Explain to students each of the calming strategies written on the board. If students don't already have a Zones Tools worksheet, give one to each student.
3. Lead the students through The Six Sides of Breathing exercise (see the handout for instructions). Practice for at least five cycles. Ask students to reflect on whether they found this calming. Have them use the worksheet to record their response about in which zones, if any, they might find this useful.
4. Draw a large numeral 8 lying on its side (lazy 8) on the board. Have students draw their own lazy 8 on a piece of paper or give each student a Lazy 8 Breathing visual. Lead students through the Lazy 8 breathing by having them trace the lazy 8 with their finger and inhale when they go around one side of the 8 and exhale when they cross over to the other side of the number. This activity also helps with crossing the midline (i.e., manipulating objects with the right hand that are placed on the left side of the body) and using both hemispheres of the brain, helping to increase body awareness and skills in reading and writing. Have them record their response on their Zones Tools worksheet.
5. Hand out the Calming Sequence visual (Reproducible U) and lead students through the Calming Sequence, repeating the routine five times. Kari Dunn Buron introduced using the meditative technique of calming sequences with students with special needs in her book *When My Worries Get Too Big* (see "Recommended Resources"). Ask students to reflect on if they think this is calming for them. Have them record their response on their Zones Tools worksheet.
6. Lead students through a counting-to-ten exercise. Using a slow, quiet voice, model for students how they can count to ten in their head with their eyes opened or closed. Explain that this gives the students time to think and make a plan before reacting. You could introduce the phrase "One hold steady, two hold steady, three hold steady, … ten I'm ready" to help students more easily learn and remember the counting-to-ten tool. Ask students to reflect on if this is calming for them. Have them record their response on their Zones Tools worksheet.

Wrap-up

Assess students' knowledge by asking the following:

How does having different types of calming techniques benefit us?

Can you think of a time over the last week that one of these techniques would have been helpful?

If you would have used a tool, how would it have affected what those around you thought about you?

Instruct students that they will continue to explore using the tools and record how the tools make them feel so that they are able to find the most effective tools to help them regulate. Have students save their Zones Tools worksheets in their Zones Folders. The lessons in the next chapter will explore ways to teach students when and how to use their tools to regulate when in the different zones.

Ways to generalize learning

- As discussed in the introduction to the chapter, it is imperative to set aside time daily for students to practice the tools. Incorporating a time to practice one calming technique a day into a daily routine will make it easier for them to continue to use them. Good times to try are after a transition from a stimulating activity, such as recess, playing, or physical education class, or before an activity that requires focusing, such as homework or a difficult class.
- Send home copies of the calming techniques and instruct parents to practice with the students once a day as part of their daily routine (such as before homework or bed).

How to adapt this lesson

- You can record answers for students if they experience difficulty writing. If a student is unable to judge in which zone the calming techniques would be beneficial, help by pointing out your observations of the student using the technique and whether or not you thought it appeared calming or alerting for him or her.
- If a student has a tool he or she already uses, make sure to include that on the Zones Tools worksheet. If a student helps create the strategy with you, they are more likely to practice it. The Six Sides of Breathing is based on an idea from a former student, and the visual and the activity were developed in collaboration with the student. He had initially made numerous self-defeating statements, such as teaching him tools was useless. However, after his role in creating The Six Sides of Breathing, he reported that he used it several times a day and it had helped reduce his time in the Yellow Zone and feelings of depression.

Additional learning activity for Lesson 11

My Green Zone Book

Have students create a book with pictures they feel are calming and would help move them back to the Green Zone. Ask students to bring in pictures from home and help them find images from magazines or the Internet that would help them feel relaxed and calm when they are in the Yellow or Red Zone. The book could include pictures of people, favorite items, preferred activities, serene landscapes, or anything else they think would be helpful. A book can be made by taking a large sheet of green construction paper, folding and cutting it into eighths, and binding an edge with staples. Have students put a title and the author (their name) on the front page. If students are able to do so, have them write captions next to each picture to explain its calming qualities. Assess students' abilities to identify calming images by evaluating the pictures they cut out before students glue them in. Students can add their Green Zone book to their toolboxes.

The Six Sides of **Breathing**

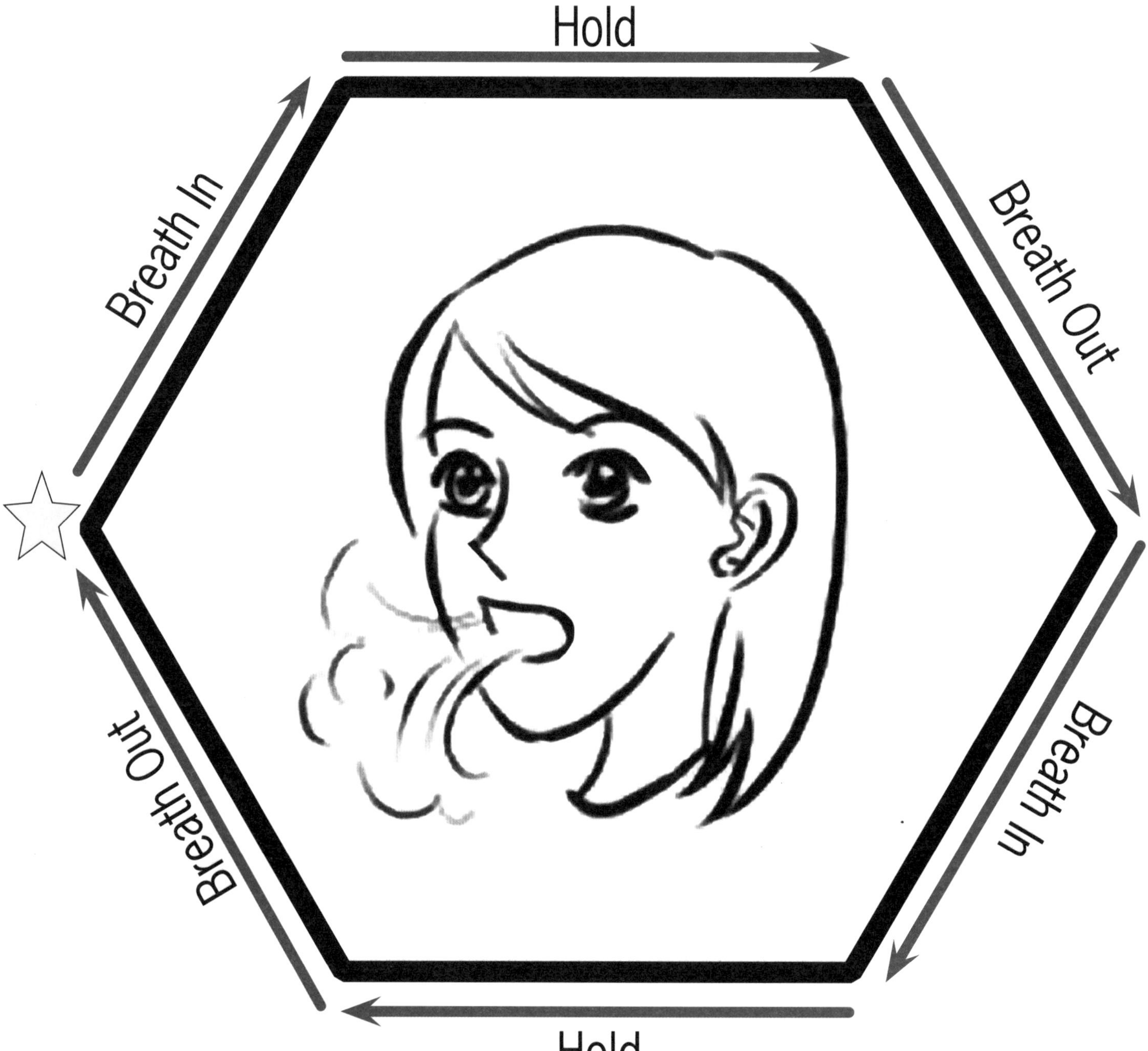

Starting at the yellow star trace with your finger the sides of the hexagon as you take a deep breath in, feeling your shoulders rise as the air fills you. Trace over the next side as you hold your breath for a moment. Slowly breathe out as you trace the third side of the hexagon. Continue tracing around the bottom three sides of the hexagon as you complete another deep breath. Continue The Six Sides of Breathing cycle until you feel calm and relaxed.

Lazy 8 **Breathing**

Trace the Lazy 8 with your finger starting at the star and taking a deep breath in.

As you cross over to the other side of the Lazy 8, slowly let your breath out.

Continue breathing around the Lazy 8 until you have a calm body and mind.

My **Calming** Sequence Visual

Activity: Try this calming sequence. Does it feel good and calming? How can you change it so that it works for you?

This calming sequence goes like this: Squeeze your hands together; close your eyes and rub your head; then rub your legs. Repeat the sequence five times, bringing your stress down.

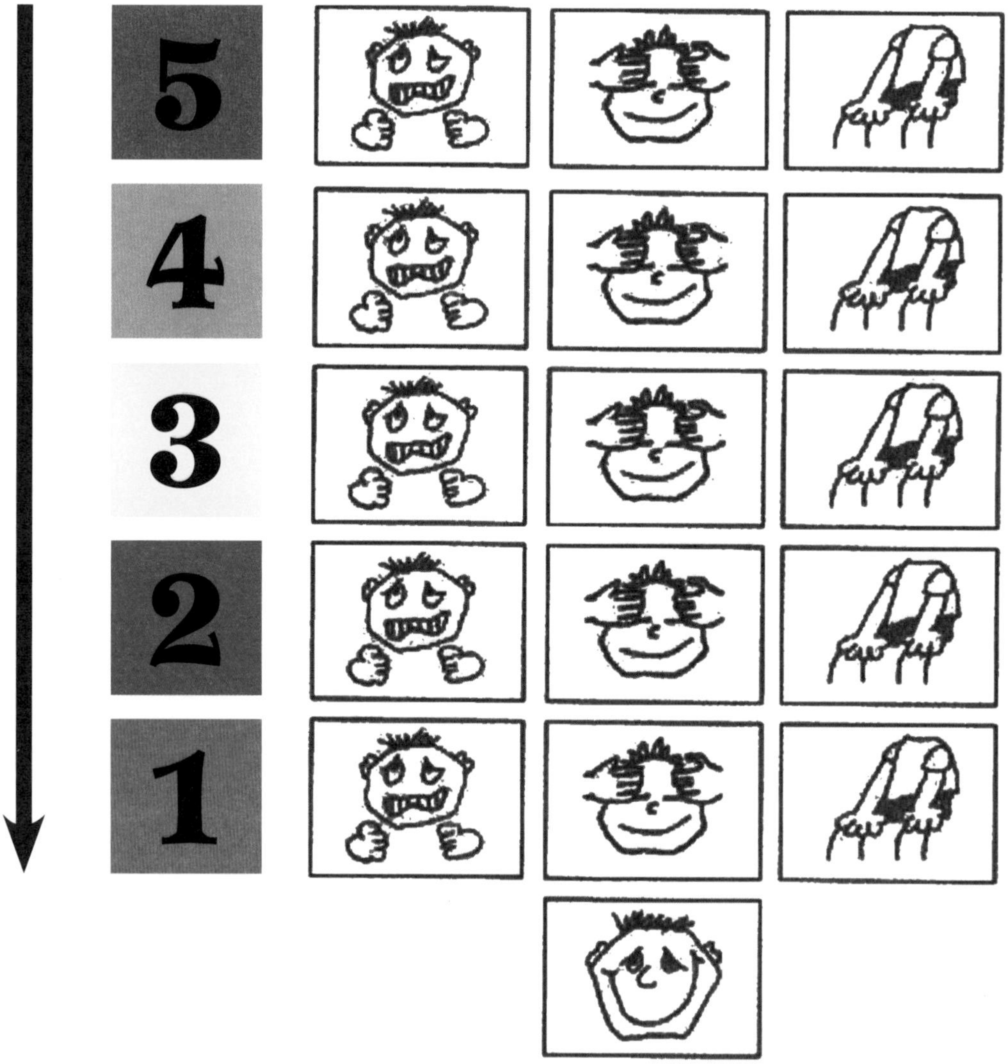

Buron, Manns, Schultz & Thomas, 2004, From *When My Worries Get Too Big!* K. D. Buron, 2006. Swawnee Mission, KS: AAPC, Reprinted with permission.

Lesson 12:
Exploring Tools–Thinking Strategies

Goals for these activities

Size of the Problem
- Students are able to provide examples of big, medium, and small problems
- Students learn to analyze a situation and rationalize how big a problem is
- Students gain insight that the size of their reaction or expected response must match the size of the problem
- Students understand how use of the Size of the Problem can help to regulate them to an expected zone

Inner Coach versus Inner Critic
- Students are able to provide examples of positive and negative self-talk
- Students demonstrate insight into circumstances when they are using negative self-talk
- Students are able to provide positive self-talk statements for circumstances they find leads them to a less regulated state
- Students understand how use of the Inner Coach can help to regulate them to an expected zone

Superflex versus Rock Brain
- Students are able to identify the difference between rigid (Rock Brain) thinking and Superflexible thinking
- Students are able to identify an instance they experienced Rock Brain thinking as well as one when they used Superflexible thinking
- Students understand that changing their thinking pattern can help regulate to a more expected zone

Overview

This lesson includes activities for three different effective thinking strategies to teach students to self-regulate: Size of the Problem, Inner Coach versus Inner Critic, and Superflex® versus Rock Brain.

With the Size of the Problem activity, students evaluate the size of problems using a visual scale and then analyze the emotional responses to those problems, looking at how some responses might be disproportionate to the level of the actual problem. The activity is designed for students to learn the basic vocabulary about the size of a problem and how it relates to the levels of emotions people experience and expect within various situations. Size of the Problem is a strategy introduced by Michelle Garcia Winner as part of her Social Thinking® learning activities. The following activity is adapted with permission for use with The Zones from her book *Think Social!* (2005) (see "Recommended Resources") and *Superflex: A Superhero Social Thinking Curriculum* (Madrigal and Winner, 2008).

By participating in a discussion and filling out worksheets, the Inner Coach versus the Inner Critic activity explores the concept of self-talk and how students can replace negative thoughts with more positive, adaptive thoughts to help them regulate. Self-talk is an executive function that is often impaired in students who struggle with self-regulation. Either students aren't aware of their inner voice or their self-talk is riddled with negative, self-defeating statements.

With the Superflex versus Rock Brain activity, students use manipulatives and discussion to explore the concept of flexible thinking versus rigid thinking. Flexible thinking is an executive function, and when students' flexible thinking pathway isn't as developed, it causes them to get stuck on one idea or one way to do something. Rigid thinking patterns often lead students to become less regulated and find themselves in the Yellow or Red Zone.

It is not recommended that you teach all of these strategies in one session; it's best to separate the lesson into three different learning activities taught on different days. Also, you may want to spend more than one session on any of these learning activities to help students solidify that concept.

Size of the Problem

Thinking Strategy Activity[7]

Materials

Size of the Problem activity:

- ☐ One Size of the Problem: Big vs. Little Problems worksheet (Reproducible V) for each student
- ☐ Copies of Size of the Problem visual (Reproducible W) to post and share with students' teams
- ☐ Students' Zones Tools worksheets

Vocabulary

What is the size of the problem?
Is it a big problem or a little problem? (These are both questions posed to help students measure the size of the problem they are experiencing.)

Big problems
(problems that many people share and that have no easy, quick, or pleasant solution)

Medium problems
(problems some people share that are able to be resolved in an hour to a couple of days)

Little problems
(problems that only affect one to two people and can be ignored or solved in a matter of minutes)

Preparation

- Copy the Size of the Problem worksheet (Reproducible V) for each student.
- Write a scale from 1-5 on the white board, with 5 on the top. Write "People see as Big Problems" next to the 4 and 5, "People see as Medium Problems" next to the 3, and "People see as Little Problems" next to the 2 and 1.
- Write the schedule on the board:
  1. Lead-in
  2. Size of the problem
  3. Wrap-up

Lead-in

Explain to students that when they participate in group activities, such as working with others on a project or playing a game together, they may get upset over what we call "little problems or glitches." For example, sometimes someone else gets something they wanted (such as the color game piece, an assigned topic to study, or being chosen first). Other times they may have an idea of how to do something, but the people they are with choose to do it a different way. We want to start working on the fact that some problems are really big while others are little and can simply be ignored. Problems require different reactions, emotions, and solutions based on their size. Tell students they will be brainstorming problems and discussing the size of each problem.

Activity

1. Explain to students that they can use the "big problem, medium problem, and little problem" strategy to help them sort out what is important to them. Associate hand gestures with big, medium, and small problems by holding your hands apart at varying distances.
2. Define what makes a problem large or small. Some of our biggest problems are problems that many people share and that have no easy, quick, or pleasant solution. Discuss what types of emotions are associated with different levels of problems and that big problems involve Red Zone reactions, medium problems involve Yellow Zone reactions, and little problems involve Green Zone reactions (which is little to no reaction).
3. Discuss how different problem levels impact a situation over time. Come up with clear examples such as how the results of a tornado can last for years (big problem) or arguing can make people upset for hours and make them feel physically bad (moderate size problem, depending on the situation). With a little problem or glitch, such as not getting

7. Size of the problem learning activity was adapted with permission from Michelle Garcia Winner's *Think Social!* (2005), pages 44-46, www.socialthinking.com.

the color game piece they want, the feeling ends as soon as the game is over and perhaps as soon as they start playing the game.

4. Have the students brainstorm different types of problems. Facilitate the students' discussion to determine where each problem fits on the scale. Examples of a 5 could include large earthquakes, being seriously hurt, or a death in the family; a 4 could include car accidents or a parent in the hospital; a 3 could include getting in a big fight with their sibling, a detention, or a suspension; a 2 could include someone taking something of theirs without asking or not doing as well as they hoped on a test; and a 1 could include not getting the color mat they want to sit on, going last, or making a mistake.
5. When determining the Size of the Problem with students, have a copy of the Size of the Problem worksheet (Reproducible V) for each student so they can write down what the class has brainstormed together on the board. An alternative is to create one Size of the Problem worksheet together as a class and then make a copy for each student.
6. Discuss how the students can start to sort out and analyze that little problems or glitches actually merit smaller Green Zone responses and reactions. Point out that this relatively quick recovery from feeling frustrated to being fine and staying in the Green Zone is what other people expect as well.
7. Using the Zones Tools worksheet, have students indicate in which zone or zones they feel thinking about the Size of the Problem would help them.

Note to Teacher

Do adapt the examples provided to fit your students' needs. Some students have more difficulty relating to society's problems as big problems because the problems do not directly affect them (such as an earthquake in another country). It is recommended that all examples are meaningful for the students and applicable to their daily life if students struggle empathizing with global or societal problems.

Wrap-up

- Discuss with students their own emotions.

  What happens when you have Red Zone responses that are at the level of a big problem when actually it was just a little problem or glitch? For example, what if you tear up your paper and storm away when you make a mistake on your work?

  If you think about using the Size of the Problem as a tool, how can it change the outcome for you (i.e., recover quickly versus not getting work done and people feeling like you overreacted)?

- The goal is to slowly work with students on understanding that their emotional response prevented them from getting their work done on time or prevented them from playing the game that they stormed away from (whatever the circumstance that may be most appropriate for your students). Have students place their Size of the Problem worksheets along with their Zones Tools worksheet in their Zones Folders.

Ways to generalize learning

- Copy The Size of the Problem visual to post where students can see it and share the visual and vocabulary with others who work closely with the students.
- This activity will establish basic vocabulary about the size of a problem and how it relates to the levels of emotions people experience and expect within various situations. Continue to use size of the problem vocabulary with students as problems occur in real time to further deepen their understanding and application of the tool. If a student reports that he or she feels it is a big problem he or she is experiencing, you can ask follow-up questions, such as, "Do you need to go to the hospital?" "Should I call 911?" or "How many people do you think we need to solve this problem?"

Size of the Problem Worksheet
Big vs. Little Problems

People see these as Big Problems	5	
	4	
People see these as Medium Prob-lems	3	
	2	
People see these as Little Problems	1	

Adapted for *The Zones of Regulation®* from the original work of Winner's *Think Social* (2005), pages 44-46, www.socialthinking.com and Buron and Curtis' *The Incredible 5-Point Scale* (2003).

Size of the Problem

Remember the size of your reaction has to match the size of the problem!

How big do others see the problem?

How big should your reaction be?

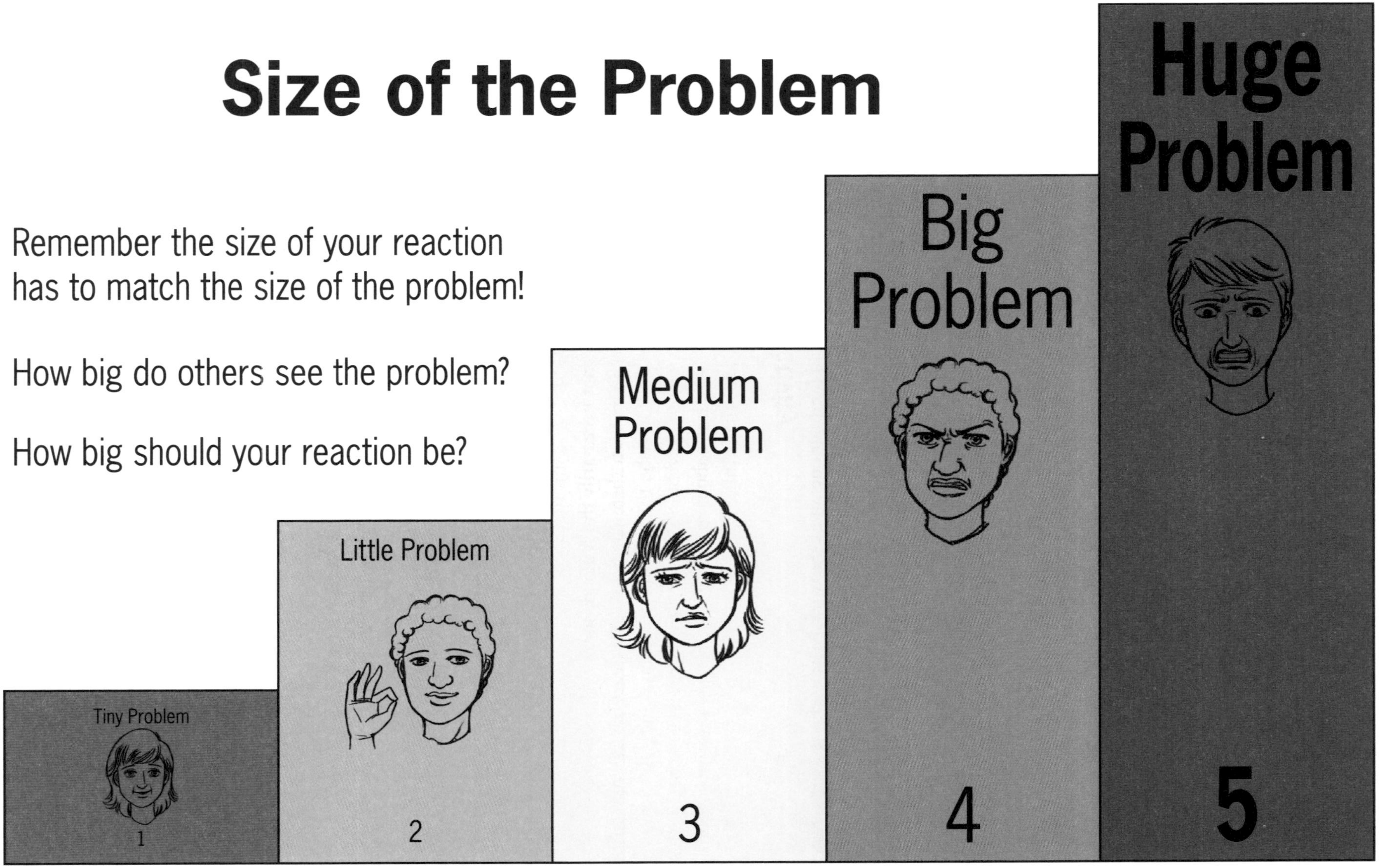

Visual adapted by Leah Kuypers, Donna Brittain and Jill Kuzma for The Zones of Regulation® from the original work of Winner's *Think Social!* (2005), pages 44-45, www.socialthinking.com, and Buron and Curtis' *The Incredible 5-Point Scale* (2003), www.5pointscale.com

Inner Coach vs. Inner Critic

Thinking Strategy Activity

Materials

- ☐ Inner Coach and Inner Critic worksheets (Reproducibles X and Y), one set per student
- ☐ Students' Zones Tools worksheets

Preparation

- Copy one set of worksheets (see Reproducibles X and Y) for each student.
- Write the schedule on the board:
  1. Lead-in
  2. Inner coach versus inner critic
  3. Complete worksheets
  4. Wrap-up

Lead-in

1. Describe to students that they all use self-talk. Ask them to consider what they would say to themselves if they reach for something in a hot oven. Usual responses would be, "It's hot," "Be careful," or "Get a hot pad." Explain that these are things they may think in their head, but not necessarily think aloud, so we call it *self-talk.*
2. Share with them the goal of this learning activity and what they will do. Describe to them that sometimes self-talk takes a negative tone, which they can call their "inner critic," and that in this activity they will learn about replacing it with more positive self-talk that they can call their "inner coach."

Activity

1. Hand out one set of the worksheets to the students. Students will first use the Inner Coach worksheet. To describe positive self-talk, teach that we all have an inner coach who helps to cheer us on and help us through difficult circumstances. Brainstorm together different things their inner coach might say to them. Instruct students to fill out their Inner Coach worksheet. You may find it easier or necessary to scribe for some students.
2. Explain that in addition to an inner coach, we also have an inner critic who works to put negative thoughts in our head, like "You can't do it; don't even try." Brainstorm together different things their inner critic might say to them. Have students fill out their Inner Critic worksheet.
3. Discuss that their brain is in control of those to whom they listen and allow to have power.
4. Using the Zones Tools worksheet, have students indicate in which zone or zones they feel the inner coach would help them.

For younger students (or to complement the activity above for elementary and less mature middle school age students)

Vocabulary

Inner coach

(used to describe positive thoughts)

Inner critic

(used to label negative, self-defeating thoughts)

Note to teacher: If you have other terms to describe positive or negative thoughts, such as the "cheerleader" and "self-defeater," it's fine to replace the vocabulary terms used in this activity with what will work best for your students.

- Rather than complete the worksheets (or in addition to doing so for students in elementary and middle school), help students reflect on the concept of self-talk by having them draw their inner coach and inner critic and give each a proper name. Help students include comics-style talking bubbles with statements from both the inner coach and the inner critic so students increase their awareness of how the critic and coach affect them.

Wrap-up

- Assess students' knowledge by asking the following:

  How can using the inner coach as a tool help you?

  Can you think of a time over the last week when using the inner coach would have been helpful? If you would have used the inner coach as a tool, would it have affected what those around you thought about you? If so, how?
- Have students place their Inner Coach and Inner Critic worksheets, along with their Zones Tools worksheet into their Zones Folders.

Ways to generalize learning

- As circumstances arise when you see students could benefit from using their inner coach, ask them what their inner coach can say to them to help them out. If you hear a student making negative, self-defeating statements, gently point out to the student that it sounds like the student is giving too much power to his or her inner critic. Remind the student to think about his or her inner coach.
- Share the worksheets and vocabulary with parents and others who work closely with the students and encourage them to also remind the students to think about their inner coach.

Inner Coach

Inner coaches help us use positive self-talk to give us the courage and strength to get through stressful situations.

Difficult times I may need my inner coach are:

____

____

____

My inner coach reminds me to use strategies to keep myself calm.

To help me get to the Green Zone, my inner coach reminds me to:

____

____

____

My inner coach also helps to keep positive thoughts in my head so I can be successful.

My inner coach might say to me:

____

____

____

Inner Critic

Inner critics use negative self-talk that get us nowhere. It puts defeating thoughts in my head.

Times my inner critic gets to me:

____

____

____

My inner critic does not help and instead ends up making a situation worse.

My inner critic might say to me:

____

____

____

I am in control of who I listen to—the inner coach or inner critic.

I can use my inner coach to defeat my inner critic by telling it:

____

____

____

Superflex® vs. Rock Brain©

Thinking Strategy Activity[8]

Materials

- ☐ A sponge or foam block (often mattress stores and factories will give out foam scraps)
- ☐ Duct tape
- ☐ Magic marker
- ☐ Students' Zones Tools worksheets
- ☐ One copy of *Superflex Takes on Rock Brain and The Team of Unthinkables: A New Beginning comic book* (optional)
- ☐ *Superflex...A Social Thinking Curriculum* (optional)

Vocabulary

Superflex Thinking

(a flexible thinking pattern in which a person is able to consider different points of view or ways to do something)

Rock Brain Thinking

(a rigid thinking pattern in which a person gets stuck on an idea and has difficulty considering other options or ways to do something)

Note to teacher: Use of the Superflex curriculum is best for students of elementary school age. It also can be used with preschool-age students who are able to grasp higher level thinking concepts and less mature middle school students. For older students, the discussion on flexible and inflexible thinking patterns can be used without applying the Superflex and Rock Brain vocabulary.

Elementary-age students can easily relate to and address cognitive inflexibility by using the concepts in *Superflex...A Superhero Social Thinking Curriculum* by Stephanie Madrigal and Michelle Garcia Winner (see "Recommended Resources"). Superflex is an entire curriculum; this activity includes an introduction to how the concept of Superflex can be used with The Zones as a tool to address cognitive inflexibility and aid in regulation. At another time, it is recommended you revisit the entire Superflex curriculum as it is an extremely valuable tool for helping students to understand Social Thinking® concepts and help further explore self-regulation.

The Superflex curriculum is based on the notion that a super hero, Superflex, lives in all of us. Superflex is always trying to defeat the Team of Unthinkables that invades our brains and tries to make us do unexpected behaviors. The Team of Unthinkables includes various cartoon characters, each designed to help students identify a different socially unexpected behavior, including the following: Glassman, who makes us have an explosive reaction; Mean Jean, who makes us say disrespectful comments to others; Energy Harry, who gives us too much energy; Brain Eater, who distracts us from what we should be thinking about and several others. As students learn about the Team of Unthinkables, you can ask them to categorize into which zone each Unthinkable puts them. Students work to increase their awareness of who is on their Team of Unthinkables and to find strategies to defeat their Team of Unthinkables through their use of their own Superflexible thinking.

Preparation

- Refer to the illustrations of Superflex and Rock Brain (see Figures 11 and 12).
  - * Draw Superflex on the sponge or foam block with Magic Markers.
  - * Wad up duct tape so that it is solid and resembles a rock. With the Magic Marker, draw on Rock Brain.
- Write the schedule on the board:
  1. Lead-in
  2. Superflex activity
  3. Wrap-up

8. The Superflex vs. Rock Brain Thinking Strategy learning activity was adapted with permission from Madrigal's and Winner's *Superflex...A Superhero Social Thinking Curriculum* (2008), pages 20-37, www.socialthinking.com.

Figure 11: Superflex®

Figure reprinted with permission from Social Thinking Publishing

Figure 12: Rock Brain©

Figure reprinted with permission from Social Thinking Publishing

Lead-in

Describe to students that they will learn to identify inflexible thinking patterns and become better at recognizing when their brains are getting stuck on something, putting them in the Yellow or Red Zone. Superflex is always trying to defeat Rock Brain, who continually tries to invade our brains and make us get stuck on an idea or way of doing something and not consider others. This often leads us quickly to the Yellow or Red Zone.

Activity

1. Explain to students that a pretend super hero, Superflex, lives in all of us. Use the foam Superflex character you made to demonstrate how Superflex is flexible and bendable (if using a sponge, make sure to dampen it first so it isn't stiff). Allow students to take turns manipulating Superflex while explaining to them that their brains are similar, as they too are flexible. Discuss how when we "change our minds" or consider several options, our brains are showing flexibility.
2. Using the character you made from the duct tape, introduce students to the concept of Rock Brain, who tries to invade our brain and make it get stuck on a thought or way of doing something. Pass around Rock Brain so students can manipulate it while asking them if they can bend or flex Rock Brain. Follow up by asking students what they think would happen if they had a Rock Brain? What zone do they think Rock Brain would put them in?
3. Demonstrate with the Superflex and Rock Brain characters how Rock Brain will try to crush Superflex (squish Superflex with Rock Brain), but Superflex is stronger and will always bounce back and defeat Rock Brain (release your hand allowing the Superflex character to expand again). Discuss with students that by thinking about Superflex, students can change their thinking pattern to consider other options and defeat Rock Brain to stay in the Green Zone. Brainstorm with students instances when they think using Superflex thinking would help them.
4. Once students understand the concept of Superflex versus Rock Brain thinking, point out that this is another tool they can use to help change their zones.
5. Have students assess in which zone Superflex thinking would benefit them and indicate this on their Zones Tools worksheet.

Wrap-up

- Assess students' understanding of the concept by asking them to respond to the following questions:

  When was a time you used Rock Brain thinking?
  Describe what happened and how it affected others.
  What do you think would have happened if you would have used Superflex thinking instead?
  How would this have changed what others thought or felt about you?
  How can using Superflex thinking affect your zone?

- Have students place their Zones Tools worksheet and any other materials related to Superflex thinking in their Zones Folders.

Ways to generalize learning

- Once students understand Superflex versus Rock Brain thinking, you can point out to them at other times when you see them using Superflex thinking to help stay in the Green Zone. Conversely, you can also let them know when you notice Rock Brain thinking that is putting them in the Yellow Zone. Ask them to call on Superflex to help them defeat Rock Brain by using flexible thinking and helping them use a tool to regain control. Given the sensitivity of the student, it may be best to process this with the student once he or she is back to the Green Zone.
- Share the concept and vocabulary with the students' parents so that they can be infused in the home and community.

Ways to Check for Learning

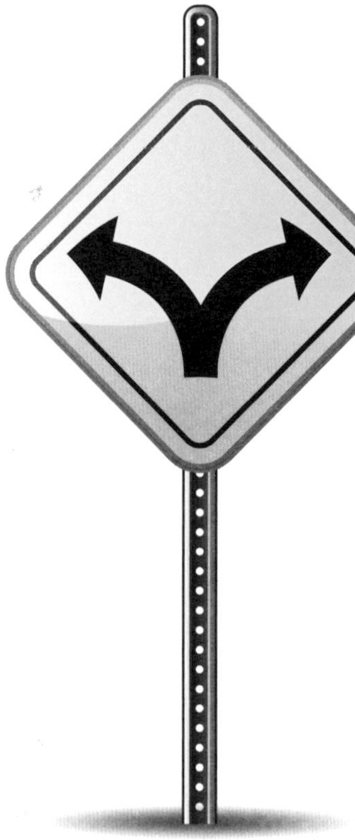

For the activities in this chapter, you can assess students' performance of tasks and the depth of their comprehension in the following ways:

- Evaluate that students sincerely participate in lessons when the tools are introduced as well during follow-up practice sessions. This is measured subjectively by your random observation.
- Look at whether student assessment of which zone a tool would benefit them aligns with your perception. This is measured subjectively through observing the student practicing the tool and then filling out the Zones Tools worksheet or by having conversations with the student.

Chapter 5:

Approaching the Finish Line

Learning When To Use and Apply Tools

In the lessons presented in this chapter, students learn how to put into practice the tools they are taught in Chapter 4 in order to change their state of alertness and regulate their emotions. Students are taught that they are in control of themselves and that to be successful, they need to know when and what strategies to use so that people around them will have more positive thoughts and feelings about them. There is also a focus on learning to be better problem solvers.

Goals for this chapter

By the end of the chapter, students will be learning to:

- Use tools to regulate themselves (Lessons 13, 14, 15, 16, 17, and 18)
- Determine when they need to use a tool to regulate (Lessons 14 and 15)
- Problem solve desirable solutions to problems they encounter (Lessons 15, 16, and 17)
- Understand how utilizing tools to regulate positively affects them (Lessons 14, 15, 16, 17, and 18)

In the lessons in this chapter, students consider the following essential questions:

- How will learning to regulate their body and emotions influence their success at home and school?
- How can understanding their emotions help identify strategies to control their behavior?
- How will the use of strategies to self-regulate influence the thoughts and feelings of others nearby?

Lesson 13:
The Toolbox

Goal for this activity

- Students understand they can engage in different strategies to change their zone and self-regulate

Materials

For younger students:

- ☐ One copy of the Zone Tools Menu (Reproducible AA) for each student
- ☐ Each student's Zones Tools worksheet
- ☐ Copy of Tools for Each of My Zones worksheet (Reproducible BB) and/or their Me and My Zones book (from Lesson 6)

For older students:

- ☐ One copy of the Toolbox worksheet (Reproducible Z) for each student
- ☐ Each student's Zones Tools worksheet

Overview

In this activity, students organize the tools they explored in the previous chapter's lessons into a visual toolbox worksheet. This allows them to have an individualized visual that they can easily refer to and display.

Preparation

- For younger students, cut apart the individual pictures in the Zones Tools Menu (Reproducible AA).
- Make copies of worksheets for students.
- Write the schedule on the board:
  1. Lead-in
  2. Create a toolbox
  3. Wrap-up

Lead-in for all ages

1. Engage students by asking the following questions:

   What do you use a toolbox for?
   What do you use the tools for?
   Why is it necessary to have a variety of tools in a toolbox?

2. Introduce the concept of the toolbox as it relates to zones and self-regulation.

   You will fill your toolboxes full of "tools" that you can use to fix or solve the problems you encounter so you can get back to the expected zone. Some of the tools you add will help to wake you up or to get out of the Blue Zone, while others will calm you down from the Red or Yellow Zone. Other tools will help you keep feeling just right, so they will be your Green Zone tools. Why do you think we want a toolbox full of strategies?

Activities for different age groups

Once the students have determined their tools for each of the zones using the Zones Tools worksheet, they should create a visual way to reference them. It is recommended that students have practiced each tool several times before they transfer it to their toolbox to allow them to reflect on the calming or alerting qualities of the tool.

For younger students

1. Have students glue pictures from the Zones Tools Menu into the zone in which they (with your input) feel it would be helpful. Students can

add zones tools to the Me and My Zones books that they completed in Lesson 6. In addition, students can complete the Tools for Each of My Zones worksheet (see Reproducible BB). The Zones Tools Menu is provided as a starting point of potential calming and alerting tools. You can use digital photographs or images from the Internet of tools to further personalize students' toolboxes.

2. Display students' toolboxes in a place that is easy for the students to reference, such as inside cover of their desk, bedroom door, or on a binder/notebook they carry with them..

For older students

- Have students transfer all Blue Zone tools from the Zones Tools worksheet into the Blue Zone section of the toolbox. Continue for the Green, Yellow, and Red Zone tools. Encourage students to add any additional tools they feel would be helpful.
- Ask students to reflect on where they would find it helpful to have it displayed (such as on their locker door or the inside cover of their planner).

Note to Teacher

If a student does not have the level of awareness or cognition needed to categorize tools, you can add tools that are tailored to that student. The finished visual can be used as a choice board offered to the student when he or she is in the different zones to help with regulation.

How to adapt this activity

Students may need a scribe if writing is difficult. Some students with cognitive challenges may not grasp the concept of the toolbox, but it is still imperative that they are taught calming strategies and that a visual system is set up so they can follow the structure of the system during times when they are less regulated. Rather than using the pictures included in the reproducible, photographs of tools used by the student (such as of a calming corner the student can access or of a sensory support the student uses such as a trampoline) or photos of the student utilizing the calming tool (for example, a photo of the student in a yoga pose) can be glued onto the Tools for Each of My Zones worksheet. Some students may be uncomfortable with having glue on their hands and prefer you to do the gluing. Also, you may find it easier or necessary to scribe for some students.

Wrap-up

Explain to students that different problems and situations are going to need tools and that is why they have a toolbox full of tools to choose from. Inform them that sometimes we use the wrong tool first, and that is okay and we continue to try one until we find what works.

- Assess students' understanding by leading the class in a discussion:

  Why is it important to use the tools that we discussed today?

  Explain how you think you will use one of the Yellow Zone tools you put in your toolbox.

  What kind of impressions will you give others when you use your tools versus going into an unexpected zone?

- Remind them that the more they use their tools, the more time they will spend in the Green Zone, making it easier to get along with others and do well in school. Ask students to store a copy of the Toolbox worksheet in their Zones Folder and remind them they can look at their toolbox as much as needed.

Ways to generalize learning

- You can display students' toolboxes in a place that is easy for the students to reference.
- Send copies of the individualized toolboxes home with the students to share with families and to refer to at home. A copy of the toolbox should also be distributed to others who work closely with each student.
- If students are using a Zones Flip Book on their desk, the tools for each zone can be taped onto the corresponding zone for easy reference.

______________________'s Toolbox

Blue Zone Tools	Green Zone Tools	Yellow Zone Tools	Red Zone Tools
________	________	________	________
________	________	________	________
________	________	________	________
________	________	________	________
________	________	________	________
________	________	________	________
________	________	________	________
________	________	________	________

ZONES Tools Menu

ZONES Tools Menu

Listen to Music

Squishes

Walk

Jumping Jacks

Shoulder Rub

Belly Breath

Inner Coach

Take a Break

Lazy 8 Breathing

Fidget Ball

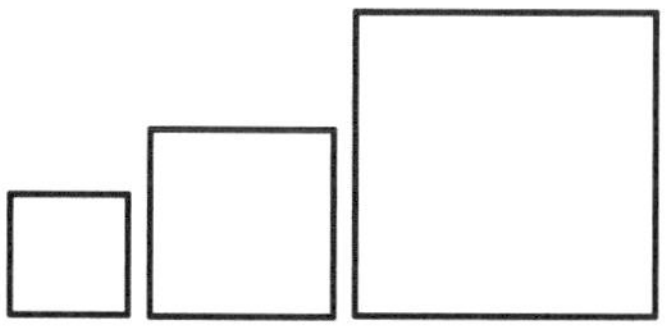

Size of Problem

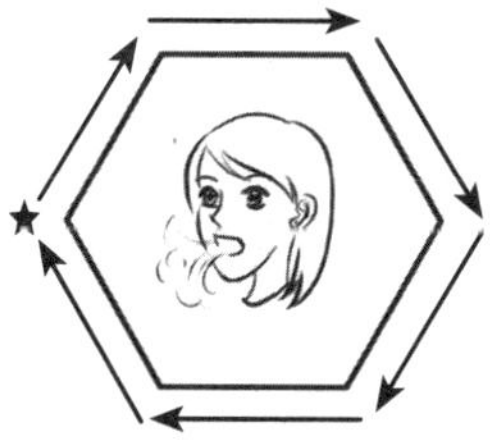

Six Sides of Breathing

 Name:____________________

Tools for Each of My ZONES

When I feel...	I can try...
Tired or Sad 	
Calm or Happy 	
Frustrated or Silly 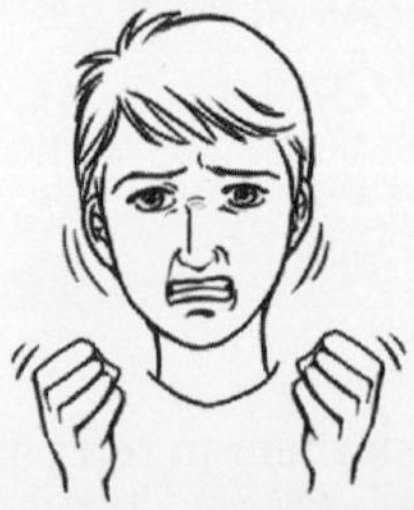	
Angry or Mad 	

Adapted for *The Zones of Regulation®* from the original work of Buron and Curtis' *The Incredible 5-Point Scale* (2003), www.5pointscale.com.

Lesson 14:
When to Use Yellow Zone Tools

Goals for this activity

- Students review what their Yellow Zone looks like in them
- Students recognize when to self-regulate and what type of tool they need
- Students understand that the more they stay in the Green Zone, the more successful they are socially and academically

Materials

- ☐ One When to Use My Yellow Zone Tools worksheet (Reproducible CC) for each student
- ☐ A pen or pencil for each student
- ☐ Role play scripts
- ☐ Dry erase markers or chalk in colors of the zones

Overview

In this activity, students participate in role plays and complete a worksheet about when to use their Yellow Zone tools. It is vital that students are aware of their early signs of becoming less regulated (for example, flushed cheeks, clenched teeth, etc.). This is critical in being able to calm down before they are carried away by intense emotions. For many of us, the physical signs of a heightened emotional state are apparent before the awareness of that emotion is processed. Therefore, it is imperative that students continue to think about and monitor what their Yellow Zone looks like so they can catch themselves before the emotions catch up to them. Parents and teachers often say that students go straight from the Green Zone to the Red Zone. However, when students learn what to look for in the Yellow Zone, they stand a better chance of "catching themselves" before they hit the Red Zone and being able to use a tool to regulate back to the expected zone.

Preparation

- Copy one When to Use My Yellow Zone Tools worksheet for each student. Replicate the worksheet on the board (minus the stop sign).
- Write the schedule on the board:
  1. Lead-in
  2. When to Use My Yellow Zone Tools worksheet
  3. Role plays
  4. Wrap-up

Lead-in

1. Share with students the goals of the lesson. Ask them to refer to their worksheets as you use the visual of the zones on the board. Have students pretend that this line depicts their zones for the day. Refer to the Red Zones and Yellow Zones and ask the students what type of tool they should use there (calming or alerting). Then point to the Blue Zone and repeat the question, ensuring that the students understand they use their Yellow or Red Zone calming strategies to calm down and their Blue Zone strategies to increase alertness.
2. Point to the peak of the Red Zone line and ask if this is where they should *first* try a using a tool. Giving them a quizzical look, point to where the Yellow Zone starts and ask the question again. Explain that they don't want to wait until they are at the height of the Red Zone to

try a tool. Stress the importance of stopping to use a tool that calms them as soon as they feel themselves moving into the Yellow Zone. Draw the stop sign at the beginning of the Yellow Zone on the board.

3. Present a scenario that a student had tried a Yellow Zone tool as soon as he or she got into the Yellow Zone, and then ask a volunteer to come up and modify the chart for the pretend day (the line would be drawn back into the Green Zone and then level out for the rest of the day). Have the other students modify their worksheets as well.
4. Engage students in a discussion by asking the following:

   How would this student's day have been different if he or she would have used a tool to stay in control as soon as he or she got into the Yellow Zone?

   As the students discuss the answer to this question, observe where the students are in their understanding of self-regulation. Stress that when they use the tools they picked out for the Yellow Zone, they are able to avoid going into the Red Zone. Have each student fill out the bottom of the worksheet to remind themselves how they feel in the Yellow Zone. You may find it easier or necessary to scribe for some students. Review with students their Yellow Zone picture in the Me and My Zones book if students have a difficult time recalling. Assess learning through evaluation of their completed worksheets.

Activity

1. Tell students they will use role plays to help learn when and how to use their tools when they are in the Yellow Zone.
   - Instruct students they first will act out the role play as written below or using a situation that the students come up with that didn't end in a positive way.
   - Next, they will work as a group to identify the best time to use a Yellow Zone tool and decide which tool or tools they think would be helpful in getting back to the Green Zone.
   - Finally, they will act out the role play a second time, but with an alternative where they pretend to use the decided on Yellow Zone tool or tools.

     Note to teacher: Depending on the size of your group, you may have to have students take turns doing the role plays or have a different set of students act out the role play the second time through. Students who are watching could video record the role play so students acting can watch themselves and further reflect on when and what tools to use.
2. Assign students to act out the following role play scenarios:
   - *You are in class for your hardest subject. As the teacher is giving the class instructions, you are distracted by another student who is making noises to himself. Before you know what is happening, the teacher is on you for not having your book open to the right page. You get your book open but*

feel lost about where to look. Then, when the teacher asks you to share your answer with the class, you lose it, slam your book shut, and storm out of class.

- *You are in P.E. class playing basketball with classmates. You have the ball and make a basket but a classmate accuses you of traveling. You didn't think you did and you get ticked off, yelling back that he is a liar. On the next play, the same classmate has the ball and you are trying to block his shot. He charges into you, knocking you down. You get up, shove him down, and the next thing you know both of you are in the principal's office.*

- *You are excited because it is Friday and you have a sleepover after school. As the day goes on, you are feeling silly and are having a hard time concentrating. In reading class you start a conversation with the person sitting next to you rather than doing the quiet reading. The teacher redirects you back to reading, but you cannot get into it. You get up and sharpen your pencil, and again the teacher redirects you to get back to your seat and to get started. You start to read but don't even remember what you have read when you get to the bottom of the page. You read it again and again but can't concentrate. The teacher asks the class to move onto the worksheet and answer the questions about what they have read. You ask your classmate for help, but he ignores you. The teacher asks students to turn in their work, but you realize you didn't get any work done.*

- *You are invited to play a game with some classmates. There are four colors of game pieces, and you start to worry about getting the red one. Unfortunately, a classmate gets red first. You start getting very irritated because red is your favorite color, and you are always red. You blurt out, "I want red!" The classmate replies, "I do too and I had first pick." You are furious and storm away.*

- *You are working on a science project with a partner. You are good at science and know exactly what to do, but your partner has his own ideas too that he keeps trying to tell you. You don't listen and keep telling him you know what you are doing, each time with a firmer tone in your voice. You both are growing more frustrated with each other and then all of a sudden you realize that you were wrong and made a mistake. Your partner snaps at you, saying, "I told you so!" You shout back at him that you wouldn't have made a mistake if he just would have shut up and let you work.*

- *You are using Legos® to build a giant structure that you have been working on for days. Your younger brother comes by and wants to play too. You don't want him to, but your parent said you have to include him. He is trying to add to your design, but instead pieces start breaking off.*

Note to Teacher

The process of students moving from practicing tools when calm to actually using a tool to regulate when in the Yellow or Red Zone will vary tremendously among students. Some will start using tools immediately and others will take weeks or months with continual support and reinforcement before they start putting tools into practice. Provide ongoing encouragement and understanding for the students. You can tell the students that learning to self-regulate is a life-long process that even we as adults are always trying to improve upon.

You are very irritated with him and yell, "You always ruin it! I'm never letting you touch my Legos again!"

3. Throughout the role plays, assess if students understand the concept of using the Yellow Zone tools early, rather than waiting until their feelings/behaviors snowball.

How to adapt this lesson

If students have difficulty role playing, you can show them movie clips that depict students having difficulty with regulation. Students can discuss when it would have been appropriate for the characters to have used a tool to regulate.

Wrap-up

Help make the lesson more meaningful for the students by telling them that it is more than likely that at some point during the next week, a time will occur when they could use a tool to help them regulate back to the expected zone. Stress that you want them to tell you when that happens, not necessarily perform the tool, though that would be great! Often students don't expect that they will become less regulated; therefore, they aren't expecting to use a tool. Have students be on the lookout for the opportunity to use a tool rather than not expecting to use one and then denying that there had been an opportunity to do so. Through dialogue, assess students' abilities to generalize the lesson to meaningful real-life situations. Have students file their When to Use My Yellow Zone Tools worksheets in their Zone Folders.

Ways to generalize learning

Once students are able to identify circumstances where they could have used a tool, ask them to set a goal for the week: commit to trying to use a tool to regulate over the next week. Ask students to share a tool they would like to try and a circumstance in which they think it could be used.

Additional learning activity for Lesson 14

Yellow or Red Zone Social Story (for younger students)

Create a Social Story (Gray 2010) or visual (see Figure 12) to help the students generalize using their zone tools across environments. This support needs to be reviewed daily so the students become familiar with the content. Individualize support for each student and consider including what tools are calming or alerting as well as how he or she may look and feel in the targeted zone. The visual can be used as a nonverbal prompt for students when they are in the Yellow or Red Zone as a means to assist them in making healthy decisions. It also can serve as a map to guide their behavior. "When I feel ______, I need to STOP and calm my body. I can try ______. This will help me feel better."

Social Behavior Map and Zone Tools (for older students)

Social Behavior Mapping (Winner 2007) is described in this book in Lesson 5. If students find it difficult to understand the significance of using a tool or feel embarrassed about it, using a Social Behavior Map will help them see the big picture of how using a tool is a lot less embarrassing than having their peers see them in the Red Zone. Fill out an Expected Social Behavior Map with the student discussing that an expected behavior is using a Yellow Zone tool when they feel frustrated, stressed, silly, or worried (whatever Yellow Zone emotion they are frequently experiencing). Then fill out the Unexpected Social Behavior Map with the unexpected behavior being not using a tool and going into the Red Zone. Once both the Expected and Unexpected Social Behavior Maps are completed, ask the student which one they would rather have their peers, teachers, and parents see. Refer to the instructions and templates for completing a Social Behavior Map included in Lesson 5: Understanding Different Perspectives.

Figure 13: Visual to help generalize use of Yellow Zone tools

 Name:______________________

When To Use My Yellow Zone Tools

In the Yellow Zone,

I look: ______________________________

____

____

I feel: ______________________________

____

____

I act: ______________________________

____

____

Adapted for The Zones of Regulation® from the original Anxiety Curve in Buron and Curtis' *The Incredible 5-Point Scale* (2003), www.5pointscale.com.

Lesson 15:
Stop and Use a Tool

Goals for this activity

- Students recognize opportunities in their day to use zone tools
- Students select an appropriate tool based on their zone

Materials

- ☐ One My Zones Across the Day worksheet from Lesson 8 (Reproducible N) for each student
- ☐ Stop and Use a Tool: Stop Signs Visuals (Reproducible DD)
- ☐ Scissors or paper cutter
- ☐ Glue
- ☐ Crayon, colored pencil, or marker in each color of the zones, one set per student
- ☐ Dry erase markers or chalk in each color of the zones

Overview

In this activity, students continue to explore when they need to stop and use a tool by relating it to their own experiences. Students complete a My Zones Across the Day worksheet and glue on stop signs at points during their day when it would have been beneficial for them to have stopped and used tools. Students also work on identifying what would have been the most effective tool at each point as well. By completing this activity, students are able to see how their day could have been different if they would have used tools to help them regulate.

Preparation

- Copy the My Zones Across the Day worksheet for each student.
- Have students' schedules available for students to copy if needed, or fill in students' schedules on the bottom of worksheet.
- Cut apart the stop signs, and distribute a worksheet and several stop signs to each student.
- Replicate the My Zones Across the Day empty graph on the board.
- Write the schedule on the board:
  1. Lead-in
  2. My Zones Across the Day worksheet with stop signs
  3. Wrap-up

Lead-in

- Tell the students that today they will look for ways they can use more tools throughout their day. Review the goals of the lesson. Ask the students:

  Why is it important to look for situations where you can use a zone tool?

Activity

1. Refer to Lesson 8, My Zones Across the Day, for instructions to give the students for filling out the graph. Instruct students to place a stop sign on the first place where they could have stopped and tried a Yellow Zone tool. Assess for accuracy before allowing the students to glue on the stop sign.
2. While at students' desks, ask them what tool would have worked well where they placed the stop sign. Ask how using a tool would have changed the thoughts of those around them.

3. Have students continue to find places where they could have used a tool, including while in the Red, Blue, and Green Zones, and report to you what tool they could have tried. Assess how students are able to pair calming and alerting tools with the correct zones.
4. After students have completed their worksheets, explain to them that it is acceptable if they have not used a tool over the last day because they are just learning how to use them. Encourage students by telling them that they are all learning how to self-regulate together. Stress the importance of helping each other out by encouraging others to use their tools and not making fun of others when people use their tools. Assure students that it is not easy to remember to use their tools, especially when they are in the Yellow and Red Zones. Emphasize that you don't expect them to remember to use a tool every time they could have, but that you hope they will gradually begin to use their tools more to spend a greater amount of time each day in the Green Zone, get along better with peers and adults, and have more success in school.

How to adapt this lesson

Refer students to their toolbox and Zones Tools worksheet for ideas for tools if students are unable to generate any. Write in their schedules at the bottom of their worksheets or glue on the stop signs if this is difficult for students. Some students may need more one-on-one assistance when graphing their zones.

Wrap-up

- Assess students' understanding of learning goals by asking the following:
  Why is it important to know which tool works when?
  How would your day have changed if you had used a tool when you indicated you should have stopped?

Ways to generalize learning

- Share students' graphs with their families and others working closely with them so everyone can help support the student with understanding when to use tools.
- Continue graphing students' zones daily, highlighting any spot where the student used a tool (you can put a star or sticker to represent using a tool). Compare and contrast with students their graphs from before they started using tools to ones later when they were more proficient at using tools to regulate.

Stop and Use a Tool: Stop Sign Visuals

Lesson 16:
Tracking My Tools

Goals for this activity

- Students increase their use of tools to aid in self-regulation
- Students generalize the use of their tools to a variety of settings

Materials

- ☐ One copy of the Tracking My Tools worksheet (Reproducible EE) for each student
- ☐ Pens or pencils
- ☐ Red and green colored writing utensil if unable to print Reproducible EE in color
- ☐ Dry erase markers in black, red, and green or chalk

Overview

Through self-monitoring using a bar graph, students discover which tools are most beneficial for them and chart the frequency of use of their tools. By completing this visual learning activity, over time students are able to reflect on the effect of their tools and find which tools benefit them most. This will help students see the positive effect of using a tool; therefore, they will be more apt to use tools with increasing frequency across environments.

Preparation

- Copy the Tracking My Tools worksheet and distribute a copy to each student.
- Draw a large-scale replica on the board.
- Write the schedule on the board:
  1. Lead-in
  2. Tracking My Tools worksheet
  3. Wrap-up

Lead-in

- Review the goals of the lesson with students. Engage students in a discussion by asking:

  How would it be helpful to keep track of our use of our zone tools?
- Instruct students that they will learn how to use a bar graph to keep track of which tools they are using and how well each tool is working (see Figure 13). Explain that by graphing their tools, they can see which tools they are using as well as how well the tools are working. Discuss that if you see a graph that is nearly empty, yet you have observed when they have had opportunities to use their tools, you can help them find ways to use their tools more often.

Activity

1. Referring to the large scale replica on the board, instruct the students that the left hand column is where they will list their favorite Blue, Green, Yellow, and Red Zone tools. The boxes to the right are to be filled in to indicate if the tool worked to help get to or stay in the expected Zone.
2. To demonstrate how to fill out the graph, take turns calling a student up to the board. While the student is at the board, have him or her write down one of the tools he or she plans to use; for example, deep

breathing. Give the student an example scenario to graph, such as the following:

> *This morning you got frustrated in computer class; you used deep breathing, and it worked. How would you fill in the graph? Over lunch it was too loud in the lunchroom; you used deep breathing to cope, but it didn't work so well. How would you fill in the graph? In science you forgot your homework and lost points, but you used deep breathing and felt better. How would you fill in the graph? Pretend that tomorrow you try deep breathing and it works again. How would you fill in the graph? And it works again the next day. But the next day, you try it and it doesn't work. How would you fill in the graph?* (Make sure the students stack the boxes they fill in, not using each box like it is a day and leaving gaps.)

3. Continue providing scenarios such as this for a number of student volunteers with their chosen tools until students demonstrate understanding in using the bar graph to keep track of their use of tools.
4. Have students list their zone tools and color in the Yes boxes green and No boxes red if the worksheet was printed in black-and-white. Scribing for students who have difficulty with printing may be necessary or easier. Have students fill in any boxes if they have completed a strategy already that day. Instruct them that this is an ongoing activity that you expect them to be filling out daily so they can see what is working for them and what is not. Let them know that you don't want to see the graph filled out with fictitious boxes. Stress that if they are filling in the boxes without doing the strategies, they are only cheating themselves by not gaining skills in self-regulation.

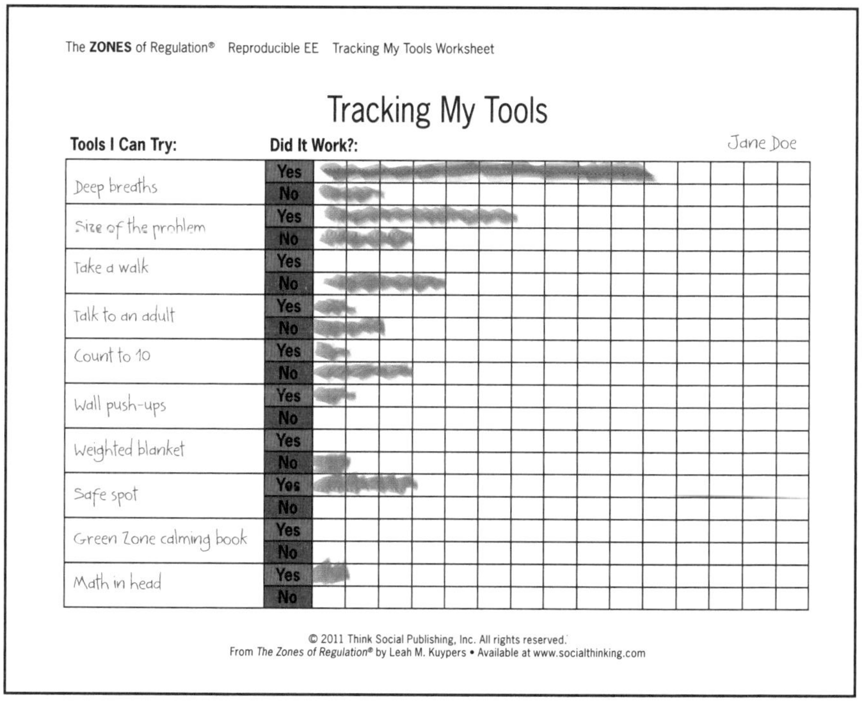

Figure 14:
Example of Tracking My Tools worksheet

How to adapt this lesson

Being able to see things from another's perspective and consider the thoughts of those around us are what motivates many of us to regulate our emotions and alertness level. We want those around us to keep thinking good thoughts about us, so we will stifle emotions or do what we need to get ourselves to a positive state; these are the lessons provided by Winner through her Social Thinking writings and curriculum (see "Recommended Resources"). Unfortunately, many students who have deficits in self-regulation have challenges in understanding how their behavior affects others' thoughts and feelings. Therefore, that intrinsic motivation to regulate around others is diminished. Many students benefit from having an external motivator tied to using a tool, *whether the tool works or not*. What is important is that the students are attempting to self-regulate, and that is a step in the right direction. You or the students' families can set up a reward system—with each attempt at using a tool, the student receives a point toward earning something that motivates them (for example, a Poké point toward a new set of Pokémon cards or a dollar toward a new video game). After the student earns a set amount of points, they get a predetermined reward.

You or an aide can graph a student's use of tools if the student is unable to do so. If students are unable to understand how the tools affect them, this activity at least serves as a guide and a data collection tool to assist staff in determining which strategies work best for students based on subjective opinion. This information can help guide staff in future interventions for that student. For older students, they can set up a graph to track their tools using a spreadsheet program on a computer.

Wrap-up

Stress the importance of using the tools throughout the week whenever they feel themselves moving out of the Green Zone. This activity is designed to provide ongoing assessment opportunities not only for staff, but also for the students by monitoring how frequently they are using self-regulating tools. It can also be used to collect data to determine the most effective tools for each student.

Ways to generalize learning

- The graph with the tools listed can be sent home or to others who work with the students for carryover in different environments.
- Weekly, if not more frequently, review the graph with students and help them identify patterns of strategies that are working and ones that are not.
- Provide encouragement when you see students using their tools and remind them to graph the results. As graphs fill and tool lists lengthen, help students recognize which tools are most effective and condense the graph.

Tracking My Tools

Tools I Can Try:	Did It Work?:															
	Yes															
	No															
	Yes															
	No															
	Yes															
	No															
	Yes															
	No															
	Yes															
	No															
	Yes															
	No															
	Yes															
	No															
	Yes															
	No															
	Yes															
	No															
	Yes															
	No															

Lesson 17:
STOP, OPT, and GO

Goals for this activity

- Students increase their problem solving and planning abilities
- Students decrease impulsive/reactive behaviors
- Students improve their ability to self-regulate
- Students work together as a team

Materials

- ☐ Individual STOP, OPT, and GO Visuals (Reproducible FF) and eight copies of the STOP, OPT, and GO Solution Finder worksheet (Reproducible GG)
- ☐ Red, yellow, and green markers, pens, crayons, or colored pencils
- ☐ Tape

Overview

In this activity, students learn a new concept, STOP, OPT, and GO, using a game format. Many students who struggle with self-regulation have difficulty with impulse control and with problem solving alternative solutions to conflicts. STOP, OPT, and GO was developed to give students an easy-to-remember phrase and visual to aid them in slowing down before they act on an impulse. Often students get stuck on one way to do something and have difficulty trying other people's ideas or alternatives. This concept helps students sort through solutions, reflecting on which solution will be most beneficial in regulating them and resolving the conflict.

Preparation

- Print a STOP, OPT, and GO Solution Finder worksheet and color it in if printing from a black-and-white printer. Post it in the classroom as a visual display. If you have a student who frequently flees the room unexpectedly, posting another on the door may be helpful.
- Write the schedule on the board:
  1. Lead-in
  2. Solution finder game
  3. Wrap-up

Lead-in

1. Review the learning goals of the lesson with students. Instruct students that they will learn how to Stop, Opt, and Go. In other words, they will learn how to stop (Stop) and consider options (Opt) before they act (Go). Ask students:

   Why do you think it is important that we learn how to problem solve to get solutions to tough problems?

2. Have students consider a stoplight. Ask them what each light of the stoplight means. Inform them that they will use a stoplight to learn how to problem solve to reach better solutions to avoid the Red Zone and improve how they get along with others. Tell the students that when they find themselves moving toward the Red Zone, they need to STOP—like when they are at a red light! While at the yellow light (in the Yellow Zone), they want to slow down and think of as many options as possible (OPT), both good and not-so-good. Remind students that while they consider each option, they need to look ahead to consider what will happen next if they choose that option. After they OPT (think

of their options), they need to GO with the best one. Inform students that they can remember this because it is similar to the fire safety slogan, "Stop, Drop, and Roll." Make them aware that if they find the option they chose is not working, they can STOP, OPT, and GO again.

3. If appropriate, have students color in smaller-scaled visuals to tape to their desk or other surfaces that they frequently view, such as planners, computers, lockers, etc.

Activity

1. Inform the students that they will work in teams to learn how to problem solve using the concept of STOP, OPT, and GO.
2. Divide the students into two teams and have the teams sit together. Ask-for a volunteer on each team to record the options the team develops. Divide the STOP, OPT, and GO Solution Finder worksheets between the two teams so each team has four worksheets. Instruct the teams that once the problem is read aloud, together they will brainstorm options to find the best solution. Each team will have a couple of minutes per problem to work together to come up with several options (good and not-so-good) and write them all down. Next, each team will decide on their best solution that will keep them in the Green Zone.
3. As a class, compare and contrast the solutions the two teams generated. If you want to make the game more competitive, keep a running tally of which team came up with the better solution.
4. Throughout the activity, assess students' abilities to grasp the problem solving concept and to generate problem solving solutions. You can assess students by observing participation and dialogue in discussions on their teams as well as with whole class discussions.
5. Have teams use the STOP, OPT, and GO Solution Finder worksheet with the problems listed below. Use as many problems as time allots, or spread out the activity throughout the week, doing a few each day. A list of suggestions is provided below or you and/or your students can create your own list of problems the students have experienced. As stated earlier, the best teachings are those that relate directly to the students' own lives.

   You lost the game.
   Your solution to STOP, OPT, and GO wasn't picked as the favorite.
   You got a much lower grade on your test than you expected.
   A classmate blamed you for something you didn't do.
   The teacher doesn't call on you when you had your hand up and knew the answer.
   There was an unexpected change in your schedule.
   A promise from your teacher was broken.
   You hate the hot lunch and didn't bring one from home.
   Too many people are talking loudly around you.
   You were late for class.

A classmate broke a minor rule.
Someone sat in your spot.
You were paired up for a project with a classmate you dislike.
Class ran late and it cut into your free time.
You caught someone cheating and it annoyed you.
Someone stole your favorite item.
A classmate isn't sharing.

Wrap-up

To help students generalize the concept into action, ask the students:

Now that you have a new tool—STOP, OPT, and GO—that can help you be better problem solvers, how can you help each other use it?

Ask students to add the STOP, OPT, and GO tool to their toolboxes and Tracking My Tools graph. Remind them to help each other use their tools and think of the stoplight next time they have a problem or feel themselves moving into the Red Zone.

Following the activity, assess how you saw the students use the STOP, OPT, and GO Solution Finder. Observe where they are having problems by considering the following: is it difficulty with stopping (controlling the impulse), developing problem solving options, or generating a satisfactory solution? Provide additional support where needed.

Additional learning activity

Continue to use the STOP, OPT, and GO Solution Finder with students on an individual basis. Ideally, this would be completed together proactively to problem solve a recurring trigger. Once the list of possible options is generated, have students cross out the options that would put them in the Red Zone with a red writing utensil, then repeat for the Yellow Zone with a yellow writing utensil. Then with a green writing utensil, have students circle the options that would keep them in the Green Zone and star the one they decide will work best. In addition, this worksheet can be used to help facilitate problem solving as a conflict occurs. Inevitably, undesired behaviors do occur despite all the proactive strategies that are put into place. When this is the case, the STOP, OPT, and GO Solution Finder can also be used to help students process better solutions for the future.

Ways to generalize learning

- Post visuals of STOP, OPT, and GO in places where the students spend a lot of time (see Reproducible FF).
- Share the strategy of STOP, OPT, and GO with other members of the student's team, teaching them how they can use it with the student to problem solve solutions (see the additional learning activity above).

Individual **STOP, OPT,** and **GO** Visuals

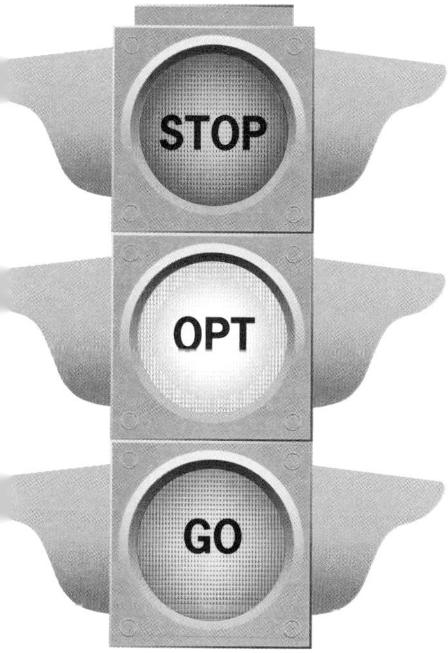

Solution Finder Worksheet

Problem:______________

Think about a situation when you had (or anticipate having) a difficult time STOPPING and staying in the Green Zone.

Use this STOP, OPT, and GO Solution Finder Worksheet to brainstorm all of the OPTIONS you have—good and bad. This includes using your tools as well as the choices that aren't so good, like losing your cool.

- Consider each option.
- Take a yellow or red marker and cross off each option that would cause you to go into those zones.
- Take a green marker and circle the best option(s) to go with.

My best option is:____

Lesson 18:
Celebrating My Use of Tools

Goals for this activity

- Students celebrate their achievements in using tools to regulate out of unexpected zones
- Students are positively reinforced for their use of tools and gains in regulation
- Students generalize their use of tools across environments

Materials

- ☐ Tool Awards! (see Reproducible HH)
- ☐ One Zones License for each student (see Reproducible II)
- ☐ Camera and equipment for printing or a class photo of each student (optional)

Overview

In this ongoing activity, you give a student a Tool Award! when you see that student use a tool, whether or not it worked. Once the student collects an agreed-upon amount of awards, he or she can turn in the awards for a Zones License. This activity is meant to help pre-school through middle school students generalize the use of their tools across environments. This creates an external motivator for students to use their tools. As they gain experience with using tools to self-regulate and reflect (with your help) on the benefits of doing so, they will move toward being more intrinsically motivated to regulate. This activity also provides a medium for students to feel proud and celebrate their successes in regulation. It is advised that vouchers are given for using a tool to stay in the Green Zone as well as for using a tool to regulate away from an unexpected zone.

Preparation

- Copy multiple Tool Awards! and trim them apart for your use with the students. Also copy multiple copies to give to parents and others who work closely with the students.
- Create a way for each student to organize their Tool Awards! (For example, they can be displayed visually in the classroom, pasted into their Zones Folder, or collected in a bin.)
- Copy one Zones License for each student.
- Take and print photos or plan to use a class picture of each student when you later create the Zones Licenses (having students draw their pictures is also an option).
- Write the schedule on the board:
  1. Lead-in
  2. Explain Tool Awards!

Lead-in

Review the goals of the lesson with students. Ask students:

Where should we be using our zones tools?
How does it feel when you use a tool all by yourself?

Activity

1. Instruct the students that they need to be using tools everywhere and will be receiving a Tool Award! when they attempt to use a tool to get to a more expected zone, even if an adult helped to remind them. Once they

collect a predetermined amount, they will then earn their Zones License. The predetermined amount may differ depending on the student. A skill must be practiced many times over before it becomes a habit, and this is something to work toward over time. Consider where the student is at for a baseline in using tools and set an amount that you feel will be a challenge but within the student's reach. Criteria options could also include with or without prompting. Refer to Lesson 16: Tracking My Tools if you feel you need more immediate reinforcements for a student as that can be used as a reinforcement schedule with fewer tools needed to receive the reward. The Zones License symbolizes that they have gained a significant amount of control and are using their tools more independently to regulate their zones. It signifies their achievement in using tools and their ability to navigate through the zones with ease.

2. Distribute awards to students when you see them use a tool or when they report to you that they did. Make sure to collect Tool Awards! from students that they received from others.
3. When a student earns the determined amount of awards to receive their license, make a celebration out of it. Paste the student's picture onto the license or have the student draw in his or her picture.

Ways to generalize learning

- Pass out Tool Awards! to other members on the students' teams so the use of tools can be reinforced across environments.
- Use this lesson in conjunction with Lesson 16: Tracking My Tools.

To help reinforce ______________________ using his or her zone tools to regulate at home, in the community, and at school, please give one Tool Award! every time the student attempts to use a tool. Even if the tool didn't work or you needed to remind him or her to use a tool, making a sincere effort to get out of an unexpected zone earns the student a Tool Award! Please have the student bring awards back to me, _____________, as we are collecting them and working toward receiving our Zones License!

Thank you for your help and support.

Tool Award!

Congratulations on using a tool from your toolbox.

Tool Award!

Congratulations on using a tool from your toolbox.

Tool Award!

Congratulations on using a tool from your toolbox.

Tool Award!

Congratulations on using a tool from your toolbox.

Tool Award!

Congratulations on using a tool from your toolbox.

Tool Award!

Congratulations on using a tool from your toolbox.

Tool Award!

Congratulations on using a tool from your toolbox.

ZONES LICENSE

For Your Achievement in Regulating Your Zones and Using Your Tools

PHOTO HERE

NAME: ______________________

HAIR: ______________________

EYES: ______________________

DOB: ______________________

AWARDED BY: ______________________

SIGNATURE: ______________________

ZONES LICENSE

For Your Achievement in Regulating Your Zones and Using Your Tools

PHOTO HERE

NAME: ______________________

HAIR: ______________________

EYES: ______________________

DOB: ______________________

AWARDED BY: ______________________

SIGNATURE: ______________________

Ways to check for learning

The following informal assessment techniques are provided as ways you can use to gauge students' understanding of The Zones concepts introduced in this chapter.

- Students utilize a strategy from their toolbox. This can be measured by random observation or by student report—orally or on the Tracking My Tools worksheet (see Lesson 16: Tracking My Tools).
- Improvements noted in students' behavior can be examined objectively by data collection, point sheets, or subjectively through observation and conversations with others who interact closely with student.
- Improved peer and adult relations and interactions can be measured by observation, student report, and reports from others who interact closely with students.

Chapter 6:

And the Winner Is…

Background Information for The Zones

Chapter 1 provides an overview of The Zones curriculum: what it is, the main influences on its development, the challenges it was designed to addressed, and more. This chapter provides additional information about the works of others that have contributed to the understanding of self-regulation and effective teaching strategies. Many of these works also influenced the development of The Zones.

How self-regulation develops

Typically, as children age and mature, so do their skills in self-regulation. Claire Kopp (1982) has provided a highly respected and widely known overview of the early phases of development of self-regulation. She puts forth a developmental progression based on theory and research that she calls "phases of control," which explains the gradual transitions that build upon each other for a person to achieve self-regulation. When considering infants and small children, it is a given that they are heavily dependent on external regulators, such as their caring parents or attentive babysitters, to meet their needs. As children age, they become more capable of handling challenging circumstances and are able to demonstrate age appropriate responses and solutions.

Kopp's first phase, called "neurophysiological modulation," occurs from birth to approximately the second or third month of infancy. During this time, Kopp explains infants have to modulate alertness states as a way to protect themselves from stimulation. Two examples of this are when babies fall asleep when in an over-stimulating sporting event or suck on a pacifier to self-sooth. According to Kopp, infants demonstrate organized movement patterns, or reflexes, during this time. Kopp's second phase, "sensorimotor modulation," starts around the third month and lasts through the ninth to twelfth month. During this time, Kopp states infants develop the ability to change their behavior in response to an event and stimuli, such as when a baby is drawn to his or her mother's activity and will reach for what the mother has just set down. When infants become aware that they can change their actions from those of others,

Kopp feels they progress into the next phase, "control." At this point, Kopp asserts children demonstrate an emerging awareness of social and task demands that are set by the caregivers. Kopp goes on to explain that children attempt to initiate, maintain, modulate, or cease their behavior according to social or task demands and begin to notice the effects of their actions. During this time, Kopp points out there is significant cognitive growth in intentionality, goal-directed behavior, conscious awareness of actions, and memory of self. Kopp continues to explain that the children's opportunities to notice the effects of their attempts at social interactions are critical during this time. Children become more aware of caregivers' wants, and guidance the children receive from caregivers helps progress them into Kopp's next phase, "self-control."

According to Kopp, children progress into the self-control phase around two years of age. During this time, Kopp theorizes children develop the ability to delay action when requested and behave according to caregivers' or social expectations despite the lack of external monitors. Kopp states that as compliance and internal self-monitoring emerge, so does the cognitive requisites of emerging language, representational thinking, symbolic thinking, and memory recall. Kopp asserts children begin to demonstrate impulse control, with the degree of success impacted by the caregivers' sensitivity to the child's needs and characteristics. Children continue to develop their sense of self and identity as they move into Kopp's final phase, "self-regulation," into which children typically progress during their third and fourth years. Around that time, they gain greater flexibility and adaptability of control processes so that they are able to change to meet the situational demands. According to Kopp, children learn to use rules to guide behavior; as children gain understanding of the standards and expectations of appropriate behavior, they attempt to shape their behavior to meet the standards. Kopp recognizes that in the phase of developing self-regulation, children learn strategies that reduce tension and increase their conscious introspection and reflection of their behavior. The skills children exhibit in this phase, however, largely depend on their ability to pick up on social cues, notice the "hidden rules" of the culture, and use self-talk.

Kopp takes into consideration the influence of external influences on the development of self-regulation. She cites various research findings supporting her theory that caregivers influence individual differences in the development of self-regulation, given caregivers' different expectations, verbal techniques, and behavior management strategies. Kopp also attests to the effect of stressful events during early childhood on the development of self-regulation.

Teaching Strategies for Students with Neurobiological Disorders

Students with neurobiological disorders (e.g., ASD, ADHD, etc.) have unique learning styles, and certain teaching strategies have been found beneficial or promising to help these students learn and apply new concepts. It is essential that we, as parents and educators, take into account these unique learning styles and teaching strategies to optimally engage all learners.

Self-management

In 2009, the National Autism Center released their publication, *National Standards Project: Findings and Conclusions*. Various experts from the field of autism reviewed literature on the wide range of treatments for individuals with autism and sought to build consensus in rating the different treatment approaches. Their mission included giving parents and caregivers of individuals with autism information on the evidence-based practices available to them; self-management was recognized as an established practice (the highest rating possible). The importance of integrating self-management (or self-regulation) into practice reflects the experts' confidence that this treatment will have favorable outcomes for individuals with autism. The experts define self-management interventions as those that involve teaching how to regulate one's behavior independently through recording occurrences and obtaining reinforcements. It also entails having individuals set their own goals. The Zones of Regulation curriculum encompasses all of these components as well as others.

Cognitive behavior therapy (CBT)

The Zones of Regulation is based upon a cognitive-behavior management framework. Cognitive behavior therapy (CBT) teaches the students about the thinking process that goes into self-regulation, helping them become more aware of their interpretations, feelings, and actions. The Zones learning activities use cognitive-behavior strategies to allow students to reflect on how their behavior affects their lives and others' lives around them. Cognitive behavior therapy is emerging in the literature as a powerful tool for teaching self-regulation to students with ADHD (Miranda et al. 2002; Riccomini et al. 2005) and ASD (Lee et al. 2007). The Zones is a cognitive behavioral approach that can be used across a student's day in the home, school, and community. By using cognitive-behavior management, the students learn how to independently self-monitor and reflect on their level of alertness and on the effectiveness of their Zone tools. This method allows students to move away from adult prompts (co-regulation) and assume personal responsibility in self-regulation.

Social Thinking and ILAUGH

Michelle Garcia Winner's Social Thinking® philosophy and approach to teaching social cognition is infused throughout The Zones of Regulation curriculum. Social Thinking teaches students to think about the expectations of varying aspects of the social world and the related subtleties of the social-behavioral expectations that are determined through a social thinking process. This is quite different from teaching students how to learn social skills through behavioral reinforcements and teaching rote social rules. Furthermore, although most emotions are involuntarily elicited, the degrees to which they are displayed depend on one's perception of social expectations and understanding of others' perspectives. Understanding our own and others' perspectives is referred to in the research as Theory of Mind (ToM) (Frith 1989). If students don't understand the social expectations and how their behaviors impact how other people think about them, they will have increased difficulty with emotional regulation.

Winner has developed the ILAUGH Model of Social Cognition (2000) — an acronym used to describe six social cognitive concepts that need to be processed and responded to within milliseconds to achieve many elements of successful interaction, including but not limited to self-regulation:

I = Initiation of Language
L = Listening with Eyes and Brain
A = Abstract and Inferential Language/Communication
U = Understanding Perspective
G = Gestalt Processing/Getting the Big Picture
H = Humor and Human Relatedness

Although all of the concepts of the ILAUGH Model are important for optimal self-regulation, I feel it is most essential for students to *understand perspective* and have *gestalt processing* (the ability to see the big picture) to independently self-regulate. Lessons from *Think Social!* (2005)—curriculum designed to teach Social Thinking for school-age students and one of Winner's numerous publications—are referred to throughout this book to assist in deepening students' understanding of social cognition. It is recommended that you use Social Thinking concepts along with The Zones of Regulation to achieve the best results.

Central Coherence Theory

Another influential theory considered when developing The Zones of Regulation was Uta Frith's Central Coherence Theory (1989). This theory describes how learners on the autism spectrum absorb the small, often irrelevant, details but have difficulty putting together all the pieces to see the bigger picture. Difficulty in gestalt thinking leads to decreased ability to recognize the source of a problem, pick up on relevant social cues, and comprehend the deeper meaning in texts. Because the zones presented here are reduced to four that are clearly defined and easy to relate to and comprehend, the students are encouraged to interpret the whole concept rather than focus on minute details. The Zones provides a concrete way to talk about the abstract concepts of emotions and states of alertness. Each lesson contains questions that can be raised to help the students connect what they are learning to the bigger picture of life. Meaningful examples are given and qualitative assessments are used to check for gestalt understanding while processing the smaller details.

SCERTS Model

An additional influence on the development of The Zones was the SCERTS® Model (Social Communication, Emotional Regulation and Transactional Support) (Prizant et al. 2006). This model refers to states of alertness being affected by social contexts (e.g., access to familiar routines and people), environmental stimulation, internal variables (e.g., feeling ill or tired), and emotional regulatory abilities. This helped make it apparent that the potential existed to teach *students* to recognize when they are in heightened states of emotional alertness as well as how to use strategies to control disruptive behavior. To achieve this, The Zones curriculum works to build skills and strategies that address deficits in emotional regulation and executive functioning. With a diverse population of students with varying needs, it was essential to develop a method to teach all components of self-regulation that could be customized and easily adaptable to each student, as well as carried over across environments by all of the people on each student's team.

Systemizing Theory

Another significant leader in the field of autism is Simon Baron-Cohen (2006) whose Systemizing Theory states that people with ASD are highly driven to create systems to understand information, including socially abstract information. Reportedly, people with ASD have a difficult time coping with changes in systems; they also have difficulty with understanding emotions and social concepts that do not lend themselves to lawful systems. For example, interstate roadway systems are concrete (literally and figuratively!) and easy to understand. Emotions and social expectations are abstract and ever-changing. The Zones of Regulation categorizes emotions and levels of alertness to develop a systematic way for the student to understand the concepts of self-regulation.

Enactive Mind approach

Because some people with ASD have the ability to solve explicit social-cognitive problems but a real-life inability to meet social demands, Ami Klin (2003) developed the Enactive Mind approach. Rather than giving the child a pre-set of rules that govern our social world, Klin argues that a plethora of factors need to be considered depending on the context and the person's motivations, needs, and ongoing adjustments. Klin cites the difficulty students with ASD have with generalizing skills to new environments as one of the major limitations of current teaching strategies. He argues that skills need to be taught in natural social settings, such as classrooms, homes, and the community rather than primarily behind closed doors. The Zones, in turn, needed to add meaning to and be applied to the student's real-life experiences, rather than just involve direct teaching in the classroom or clinic. The Zones' learning activities reinforce student application of the concepts in all areas of their lives; real-life opportunities to practice and apply The Zones are encouraged throughout the curriculum. It is essential to have parents, teachers, and others who work closely with the students help the students apply The Zones concepts across environments.

Research on reinforcers and point systems

Marks, Hudson, Schrader, Longaker, & Levine (2006), who also study behavior management techniques, report that losing high-interest reinforcing activities (e.g., a student is obsessed with a comic book and is punished by having it taken away) and using individual point systems are not determined to be effective in modifying student's behavior, nor are they considered best practices in behavior management with students with ASD. On the contrary, Marks et al. report that students with ASD are driven to be perfectionists, and working toward a reward that is too highly desired can increase anxiety, strengthen obsessions, and cause significant disruptions if not earned. Rather, students should work toward rewards that are desirable but not all-consuming for the student.

See the Bibliography in the Appendix for reference information about the works discussed here.

Appendix

Frequently Asked Questions

Can someone be in more than one zone at a time?

Yes. A student may feel tired (blue) because she didn't get enough sleep yet anxious (yellow) at the same time due to an upcoming test. Students do not need to pick one zone. If they list more than one zone, it indicates that they are really in touch with their feelings and alertness level. Also, the same emotion can be categorized into different zones. For example, "disappointed" could be in the Blue or Yellow Zone and "jealous" could be in the Red or Yellow Zone; the zone depends on the intensity of the emotion.

Should students be penalized for being in the Red Zone?

It's best for students to experience the natural consequences of being in the Red Zone. If students' actions while in the Red Zone hurt others or destroy property, the students need to repair their relationships and take responsibility for any property damage or messes they made. Once they have calmed down, you can use the circumstances of when they went into the Red Zone as a learning opportunity to process what they would do differently next time (see the Lesson 17: STOP, OPT and GO Additional learning activity). Additionally, it's best not to reward students for staying in the Green Zone, as it is not always the expected zone (see below). If you set up a reward system based on regulation, make sure to give praise/rewards when students make attempts to manage their Zones, even if they are not successful. If students are frequently in the Red Zone, parents and teachers need to look at the situation that was the catalyst for the student going into the Red Zone. Are there environmental accommodations that can be made or a set of sensory tools set up to help the student be more successful? Make sure you are pre-teaching tools that students can utilize to help them navigate away from their tendency to go into the Red Zone. Students also get a lot of attention, despite it being negative, for going into the Red Zone. Make sure you are teaching positive ways of getting attention, for example, using verbal strategies such as "I need help." Also, do give positive attention to the students for attempts made and even small successes.

Can you look like one zone on the outside and feel like you are in another on the inside?

Yes. It appears that many of us "disguise" our zone to match the social expectations. We use the expression, "put on a happy face" or mask the emotion so we keep people having good thoughts about us. In school, many students put everything they have into trying to stay in the Green Zone, but inside . . . the Yellow Zone is brewing. Parents frequently say that their son or daughter "loses it" and goes into the Red Zone as soon as the parents pick up the student after school. This indicates that the student is increasing his or her awareness of peers and is making every effort to hold it together so the peers continue to think good thoughts about that child. The student feels safe in the car with parents and then lets it all out. You can emphasize to these students that they need to manage the Yellow Zone inside of them throughout the day so it doesn't turn into the Red Zone. Great tools for doing this include yoga, Brain Gym® (see "Appendix C: Recommended Resources"), exercise, and mental breaks.

How does The Zones of Regulation differ from the Alert Program?

The Alert Program® is an excellent curriculum and the leader in the field in addressing self-regulation through the use of sensory supports and activities that work to regulate the nervous system. Using a cognitive behavior approach like that used in The Zones of Regulation, the Alert Program has led the way for occupational therapists, parents, and other professionals in giving students a friendly language to identify their level of alertness. It provides a variety of lessons for students to explore this concept. The Zones is the next step in the process, as it addresses emotional regulation, skill building in executive functioning, and social cognition. The Zones curriculum is designed to help students become aware of their emotions and how emotions and thinking patterns as well as sensory needs impact alertness levels. In addition, with The Zones, students gain insight into social expectations and understanding that their feelings and level of alertness need to match the social demands of the environment they are in. The Zones of Regulation teaches tools such as calming techniques and thinking strategies that can be used in addition to sensory tools to regulate. Students who use the Alert Program can incorporate their engine tools into their Zones Toolbox and the language from both concepts can be used together: "It looks like your engine is running high and you are in the Yellow Zone. What is a tool that will help you feel just right and get back to the Green Zone?"

How does The Zones of Regulation differ from the Incredible 5-Point Scale?

The Incredible 5-Point Scale is one of the key tools that inspired the evolution of The Zones of Regulation. It is an amazing strategy to break down any skill or behavior into five degrees or smaller parts so that students can better understand the subtleties of a behavior and think of it in concrete terms. Both the 5-Point Scale and The Zones of Regulation are cognitive behavior approaches that use a system to help teach students the range of a behavior and what it looks and feels like. The 5-Point scale can be used to teach emotional regulation or self control and also for a plethora of other behaviors. Based on this scale, it is now a common practice in schools to break down voice volume into five levels, ranging from not talking to screaming. Other ideas for application of a 5-point scale include personal space, anxiety, anger, obsessions, and body language. Ultimately, using a 5-point scale helps students to learn to be aware of and regulate a behavior. The Zones of Regulation differs in that it is a curriculum designed to teach the underlying skills in being able to self-regulate. As such, it includes numerous lessons and learning activities to teach students to be aware of and regulate their emotions and sensory needs, understand the perspectives of others, control their impulses, and be better problem solvers.

The Zones and the Incredible 5-Point scale can be integrated to work together. If you are using a 5-point scale for emotional regulation and want to expand on it with The Zones learning activities, help students be flexible by reassigning the colors. You can call a 4-5 on the scale the Red Zone, a 3 the Yellow Zone, and a 1-2 the Green Zone, and add in the Blue Zone below the scale (you could assign a 0 to it). Students can continue to refer to the numbers they know, as well as relate them to the zone colors. This way learning activities from The Zones curriculum can be adapted to fit into the 5-point scale the students are familiar with. We just all need to be flexible thinkers!

What do I do if the student doesn't want to do The Zones?

If a student complains, "Why am I the only one who has to do The Zones?," first take a look at two things. Are you only pointing out when the student is in the unexpected zones and not giving enough praise to the student for maintaining or regulating to the expected zone? Second, have you sufficiently created the culture of The Zones so the student sees that we all become less regulated and in an unexpected zone from time to time and use tools to manage their Zones? You can encourage students to sit at a playground, public pool, or mall and see if they can detect the zones in others around them. You can then discuss with students how the zones are in everyone.

Another great resource is the SCERTS® Model, which provides a course of action to aid students to become more competent and confident in their social communication (SC). It also works to eliminate problem behaviors that impede student learning and their ability to forge meaningful relationships (ER for emotional regulation). Transactional supports (TS) help families, educators, and therapists collaborate as a team to ensure the utmost progress for the student. By addressing these supports, those working closely with the student work to develop and implement tools to better support that student. This enables them to be in sync with the student's needs and interests, modify and adapt the environment, and provide strategies to boost learning (for example, The Zones, picture communication, visual schedules, and sensory supports). In the spirit of collaboration, individualized student plans are also created to provide support and education to families and promote teamwork among all those working closely with the student.

Proposed IEP Goals for Building Self-Regulation

These are suggestions. Please adapt them as appropriate for each student.

Student will increase emotional vocabulary as demonstrated by labeling emotions __________, __________, and __________ in self and others with __________ accuracy.

Student will increase ability to understand body language as demonstrated by identifying __________ different facial expressions in pictures and model on self with __________ accuracy.

Given potential real-life scenarios, student will increase perspective taking skills as demonstrated by categorizing what the expected state (or zone) would be for each scenario with __________ accuracy.

Student will increase perspective taking skills as demonstrated by reflecting on how his or her behavior in a given circumstance impacted the thoughts and feelings of those near him or her on three given occasions with __________ accuracy.

Student will increase awareness of his or her states of alertness and emotions (or zones) as demonstrated by identifying __________ physiological characteristics (for example, stomach pain, clenched fists, muscles relaxed, mind racing) unique to each of his or her four zones with __________ accuracy.

Student will increase awareness of his or her state of alertness and emotions as demonstrated when the emotional/alertness state (zone or feeling) the student reports matches the teacher's assessment with __________ accuracy.

Student will improve his or her regulation skills as demonstrated by identifying __________ triggers that cause a loss of regulation for himself or herself with __________ accuracy.

Student will improve insight on regulation as demonstrated by identifying the instances over the course of his day where he or she could have benefited from utilizing a tool to aid in regulation and determine what tool would have been beneficial for each instance with __________ accuracy.

Student will improve insight on regulation as demonstrated by describing how his or her day would have been different (that is, relationships with peers, success in school) if he or she would have utilized a tool to aid in regulation for __________ out of __________ opportunities.

Student will improve his or her regulation skills as measured by being able to list and demonstrate __________ tools he or she finds calming (Yellow and Red Zone tools), __________ tools that help keep him or her feeling calm (Green Zone tools), and __________ tools that help wake him or her up (Blue Zone tools).

Student will improve problem solving skills as demonstrated by brainstorming both positive and negative solutions to a conflict and determining the optimal solution to resolve the conflict __________ out of __________ opportunities.

Student will improve regulation skills as demonstrated by stopping self with one verbal prompt when acting on impulse and carry out an expected behavior for __________ out of __________ opportunities.

Student will improve his or her regulation skills as demonstrated by responding to a (verbal, visual, gestural) prompt to utilize a tool to aid self in regulating to an expected state (or zone), __________ out of __________ opportunities.

Student will improve his or her self-regulation skills as demonstrated by independently utilizing a tool to aid self in regulating to an expected state (or zone), __________ out of __________ opportunities.

Recommended Resources

Children's Literature for Classroom Use

- *How Do I Feel? An Interactive Reading Book of Emotions I Have Feelings, Too! An Interactive Reading Book of Emotions for Teens, Adults and Seniors*
  By Joan Green and illustrated by Linda Comerford, Greenhouse Publications (2006)
- *Miss Nelson Is Missing*
  By Harry Allard and James Marshall, Houghton Mifflin Company (1977)
- *No, David!*
  By David Shannon, The Blue Sky Press (1998)
- *On Monday When It Rained*
  By Cherryl Kachenmeister, Houghton Mifflin Sandpiper Books (2001)
- *The Way I Feel*
  Written and illustrated by Janan Cain, Parenting Press (2000)
- *Today I Feel Silly & Other Moods That Make My Day*
  By Jamie Lee Curtis, HarperCollins (1998)
- *When Sophie Gets Angry—Really, Really Angry. . .*
  By Molly Bang, The Blue Sky Press (1999)
- *Whole Body Listening Larry at School*
  By Elizabeth Sautter and Kristen Wilson, Social Thinking Publishing (2011)

Movies

- *Charlie Brown* movies or TV specials,
  By Charles Schultz
  Available from local libraries, video rental stores, or www.amazon.com
- *Finding Nemo,* Disney (2003)
  Available from local libraries, video rental stores, or www.amazon.com
- *The Outsiders*, Zoetrope Studios (1983)
  Available from local libraries, video rental stores, or www.amazon.com
- *Winnie the Pooh* movies, Disney
  Available from http://disney.go.com/pooh/html/products/index.html and local libraries, video rental stores, or www.amazon.com

Visual Supports

- Boardmaker® by Mayer-Johnson LLC, DynaVox Mayer-Johnson
  2100 Wharton Street Suite 400
  Pittsburgh, PA 15203
  Phone: 800-588-4548
  Fax: 866-585-6260
  Email: mayer-johnson.usa@mayer-johnson.com
  www.mayer-johnson.com
- SticKids™ (2005) by Community Therapy Associates, 41050 Camden Lane
  Box 6, Site 5, RR 1 Cochrane, AB, Canada
  http://stickids.com/index.html
- Jill Kuzma's SLP Social & Emotional Skill Sharing Site
  http://jillkuzma.wordpress.com

Supplemental Curriculum and Approaches

- *The Anxiety Cure for Kids*
  By Elizabeth DuPont Spencer, Robert L. DuPont, and Caroline M. DuPont, Wiley (2003)
  Available from www.amazon.com
- *Brain Gym®*
  Brain Gym is a program of physical movements that enhance learning and performance in all areas through enjoyable activities that integrate the body and mind. www.braingym.org

- *Exploring Feelings (Anxiety and Anger)*
  By Tony Attwood, Future Horizons, Inc. (2004) www.tonyattwood.com.au
- *The Explosive Child*
  Treating the Explosive Child
  Teaches the use of the Collaborative Problem Solving approach to use with easily frustrated and chronically inflexible children. By Ross Greene, HarperCollins (2005) www.livesinthebalance.org
- *How Does Your Engine Run?® A Leader's Guide to the Alert Program® for Self-Regulation*
  By Mary Sue Williams and Sherry Shellenberger, Therapy Works, Inc. (1996)
  www.alertprogram.com
- *The Incredible 5-Point Scale*
  Assisting Students with Autism Spectrum Disorders in Understanding Social Interactions and Controlling Their Emotional Responses By Kari Dunn Buron and Mitzi Curtis, Autism Asperger Publishing Co. (2003) www.5pointscale.com
- *When My Worries Get Too Big! A Relaxation Book for Children Who Live With Anxiety* By Kari Dunn Buron, Autism Asperger Publishing Co. (2006) www.5pointscale.com
- *Comic Strip Conversations*
  By Carol Gray, Future Horizons (1994)
  www.thegraycenter.org
- *The New Social Stories Book: 10th Anniversary Edition*
  By Carol Gray, Future Horizons (2010)
  www.thegraycenter.org
- *Superflex®: A Superhero Social Thinking® Curriculum*
  By Stephanie Madrigal and Michelle Garcia Winner, Social Thinking Publishing (2008)
  www.socialthinking.com
- *Think Social! A Social Thinking® Curriculum for School-Age Students*
  By Michelle Garcia Winner, Social Thinking Publishing (2005) www.socialthinking.com
- *Thinking About You Thinking About Me, 2nd Edition*
  By Michelle Garcia Winner, Social Thinking Publishing (2007) www.socialthinking.com
- *The Kids' Yoga Deck*
  By Annie Buckley, Chronicle Books (2006)
  Available from www.amazon.com
- *The Out-Of-Sync Child: Recognizing and Coping With Sensory Processing Disorder, 2nd Edition*
  By Carol S. Kranowitz, Perigee (2005)
  www.out-of-sync-child.com/publications.htm
- *Sensational Kids: Hope and Help for Children with Sensory Processing Disorder*
  By Lucy Jane Miller, Putnam Adult (2006)
  www.spdfoundation.net
- *Smart but Scattered*
  The Revolutionary "Executive Skills" Approach to Helping Kids Reach Their Potential
  By Peg Dawson and Richard Guare, Guilford Press (2009)

Planning Tools

- *The SCERTS® Model: A Comprehensive Educational Approach for Children with Autism Spectrum Disorders*
  By Barry Prizant, Amy Wetherby, Emily Rubin, Amy Laurent, and Patrick Rydell, Paul H. Brooks Publishing Co. (2006) www.scerts.com
- *The Ziggurat Model: A Framework for Designing Comprehensive Interventions for Individuals With High-Functioning Autism and Asperger Syndrome*
  By Ruth Aspy, Ph.D. and Barry G. Grossman, Ph.D., Autism Asperger Publishing Company (2007) www.texasautism.com
- *The Comprehensive Autism Planning System (CAPS) for Individuals with Asperger Syndrome, Autism and Related Disabilities*
  By Shawn Henry and Brenda Smith Myles, Autism Asperger Publishing Company (2007)
  www.aapcpublishing.net

Bibliography

American Psychiatric Association. (1994). *Diagnostic and statistical manual of mental disorders (4th ed.).* Washington, DC: Author.

Amaral, D. (2008, May). *An overview of current research on autism spectrum disorders.* Lecture presented at the Minnesota Autism Symposium, Minneapolis, MN.

Attwood, T. (2004). *Exploring feelings: anger.* Arlington, TX: Future Horizons, Inc.

Attwood, T. (2004). *Exploring feelings: anxiety.* Arlington, TX: Future Horizons, Inc.

Ayres, A. J. (1972). *Sensory integration and learning disorders.* Los Angeles, CA: Western Psychological Services.

Ayres, A. J. (1979). *Sensory integration and the child.* Los Angeles, CA: Western Psychological Services.

Barkley, R. A. (1997). Behavioral inhibition, sustained attention, and executive functions: Constructing a unifying theory of ADHD. *Psychological Bulletin, 121*(1), 65-94.

Baron-Cohen, S. (2006). The hyper-systemizing, assortative mating theory of autism. *Progress in Neuro-Psychopharmacology & Biological Psychiatry, 30*(5), 865-872.

Bieberich, A. A., & Morgan, S. B. (2004). Self-regulation and affective expression during play in children with autism or down syndrome: A short-term longitudinal study. *Journal of Autism and Developmental Disorders, 34*(4), 439-448.

Bronson, M. (2000). *Self-regulation in early childhood.* New York: The Guilford Press.

Buron, K. D. (2006). *When my worries get too big!: A relaxation book for children who live with anxiety.* Shawnee Mission, KS: Autism Asperger Publishing Co.

Buron, K. D., & Curtis, M. (2003). *The incredible 5-point scale.* Shawnee Mission, KS: Autism Asperger Publishing Co.

Byers, R. (1999). Experience and achievement: Initiatives in curriculum development for pupils with severe and profound and multiple learning difficulties. *British Journal of Special Education, 26*(4), 184-188.

Cain, J. (2000). *The way I feel.* Seattle, WA: Parenting Press, Inc.

Dawson, P., & Guare, R. (2009). *Smart but Scattered.* New York: The Guilford Press.

Degangi, G. A., Breinbauer, C., Roosevelt, J. D., Porges, S., & Greenspan, S. (2000). Prediction of childhood problems at three years in children experiencing disorders of regulation during infancy. *Infant Mental Health Journal, 21*(3), 156-175.

Department of Children Families & Learning. (2001). *Integrating Minnesota graduation standards and special education: A framework.* Roseville, MN: Author.

Dodge, K. A. (1989). Coordinating responses to aversive stimuli: Introduction to a special section on the development of emotion regulation. *Developmental Psychology, 25*(3), 339-342.

Egger, H. L., & Angold, A. (2006). Common emotional and behavioral disorders in preschool children: Presentation, neurology, and epidemiology. *Journal of Child Psychology & Psychiatry, 47*(3), 313-337.

Fisher, N., & Happé, F. (2005). A training study of theory of mind and executive function in children with autistic spectrum disorders. *Journal of Autism and Developmental Disorders, 35*(6), 757-771.

Gomez, C. R., & Baird, S. (2005). Identifying early indicators for autism in self-regulation difficulties. *Focus on Autism and Other Developmental Disabilities, 20*(2), 106-116.

Grandin, T., & Scariano, M. (1986). *Emergence: Labeled autistic.* New York: Warner Books.

Green, J. (2004). *I have feelings, too! An interactive reading book of emotions for teens, adults and seniors.* Santa Clarita, CA: Greenhouse Publications.

Greene, R. W. (2005). *The explosive child.* New York, NY: HarperCollins Publishers.

Greene, R. W., & Ablon, J. S. (2006). *Treating explosive kids: The collaborative problem-solving approach.* New York, NY: The Guilford Press.

Greene, R. W. (1998). *The explosive child: A new approach for understanding and parenting easily frustrated, "chronically inflexible" children*. New York, NY: HarperCollins Publishers.

Greene, R. W., Ablon, J. S., Goring, J. C., Raezer-Blakely, L., Markey, J., Monuteaux, M. C., et al. (2004). Effectiveness of collaborative problem solving in affectively dysregulated children with oppositional-defiant disorder: Initial findings. *Journal of Consulting and Clinical Psychology, 72*(6), 1157-1164.

Greene, R. W., Ablon, J. S., Hassuk, B., Regan, K. M., & Martin, A. (2007). "Use of collaborative problem solving to reduce seclusion and restraint in child and adolescent inpatient units": Correction. *Psychiatric Services, 58*(8), 1040.

Greene, R. W., Ablon, J. S., & Martin, A. (2006). Use of collaborative problem solving to reduce seclusion and restraint in child and adolescent inpatient units. *Psychiatric Services, 57*(5), 610-612.

Greene, R. W., Biederman, J., Faraone, S. V., Sienna, M., & Garcia-Jetton, J. (1997). Adolescent outcome of boys with attention-deficit/hyperactivity disorder and social disability: Results from a 4-year longitudinal follow-up study. *Journal of Consulting and Clinical Psychology, 65*(5), 758-767.

Happé, F. (1994). *Autism: An introduction to psychological theory.* Cambridge, MA: Harvard University Press.

Happé, F., Booth, R., Charlton, R., & Hughes, C. (2006). Executive function deficits in autism spectrum disorders and attention-deficit/hyperactivity disorder: Examining profiles across domains and ages. *Brain and Cognition, 61*(1), 25-39.

Happé, F., & Frith, U. (2006). The weak coherence account: Detail-focused cognitive style in autism spectrum disorders. *Journal of Autism and Developmental Disorders, 36*(1), 5-25.

Harris, C. R., Kaff, M. S., Anderson, M. J., & Knackendoffel, A. (2007). Designing flexible instruction. *Principal Leadership, 7*(9), 31-35.

Henderson, H. A., & Wachs, T. D. (2007). Temperament theory and the study of cognition-emotion interactions across development. *Developmental Review, 27*(3), 396-427.

Henry, S. & Smith, B. (2007). *The Comprehensive Autism Planning System (CAPS) for Individuals with Asperger Syndrome, Autism and Related Disabilities.* Shawnee Mission, KS: Autism Asperger Publishing Company.

Janzen, J. E. (2003). *Understanding the nature of autism: A guide to the autism spectrum disorders* (2nd ed.). San Antonio, TX: Harcourt Assessment, Inc.

Kachenmeister, C. (1989). *On Monday when it rained.* Boston: Houghton Mifflin Company.

Kats-Gold, I., Besser, A., & Priel, B. (2007). The role of simple emotion recognition skills among school aged boys at risk of ADHD. *Journal of Abnormal Child Psychology, 35*(3), 363-378.

Kopp, C. B. (1982). Antecedents of self-regulation: A developmental perspective. *Developmental Psychology, 18*(2), 199-214.

Kranowitz, C. S. (2005). The *out-of-sync child: recognizing and coping with sensory processing disorder.* New York, NY: Penguin Group

Lee, S., Simpson, R. L., & Shogren, K. A. (2007). Effects and implications of self-management for students with autism: A meta-analysis. *Focus on Autism and Other Developmental Disabilities, 22*(1), 2-13.

Lewis, M. D., & Todd, R. M. (2007). The self-regulating brain: Cortical-subcortical feedback and the development of intelligent action. *Cognitive Development, 22*(4), 406-430.

Liebermann, D., Giesbrecht, G. F., & Muller, U. (2007). Cognitive and emotional aspects of self-regulation in preschoolers. *Cognitive Development, 22*(4), 511-529.

Lloyd, J. W., Forness, S. R., & Kavale, K. A. (1998). Some methods are more effective than others. *Intervention in School and Clinic, 33*(4), 195-200.

Loth, E., Gómez, J. C., & Happé, F. (2008). Event schemas in autism spectrum disorders: The role of theory of mind and weak central coherence. *Journal of Autism and Developmental Disorders, 38*(3), 449-463.

Madrigal, S., Winner, M. G. (2008). *Superflex: a superhero social thinking curriculum.* San Jose, CA: Social Thinking Publishing.

Marks, S., Hudson, J., Schrader, C., Longaker, T., & Levin, M. (2006). Reconsidering behavior management for students with autism spectrum disorders. *Beyond Behavior, Winter.*

McTighe, J., & Wiggins, G. (2004). *Understanding by design: Professional development workbook.* Alexandria, VA: Association for Supervision and Curriculum Development.

McTighe, J., & Wiggins, G. (2005). *Understanding by design: Expanded 2nd ed.* Alexandria, VA: Association for Supervision and Curriculum Development.

Mesibov, G. B., Shea, V., & Schopler, E. (2004). *The TEACCH approach to autism spectrum disorders.* New York: Springer Science+Business Media, LLC.

Miller, L. J. (2006). *Sensational kids: hope and help for children with sensory processing disorder.* New York, NY: Penguin Group.

Minnesota Department of Education. (2008, September 22). *Minnesota academic standards: Mathematics k-12 (2007 version).* Retrieved October 3, 2008, from http://education.state.mn.us/MDE/Academic_Excellence/Academic_Standards/index.html

Minnesota Department of Education. (2003, May 19). *Minnesota academic standards: Language arts k-12.* Retrieved October 3, 2008, from http://education.state.mn.us/MDE/Academic_Excellence/Academic_Standards/index.html

Miranda, A., Presentación, M. J., & Soriano, M. (2002). Effectiveness of a school-based multicomponent program for the treatment of children with ADHD. *Journal of Learning Disabilities, 35*(6; 6), 546.

Murray-Slutsky, C., & Paris, B. A. (2000). *Exploring the spectrum of autism and pervasive developmental disorders: Intervention strategies.* Austin, TX: Hammill Institute On Disabilities.

Myles, B. S., Cook, K. T., Miller, N. E., Rinner, L., & Robbins, L. A. (2000). *Asperger syndrome and sensory issues.* Shawnee Mission, KS: Autism Asperger Publishing Co.

Myles, B. S., Grossman, B. G., Aspy, R., Henry, S. A., & Coffin, A. B. (2007). Planning a comprehensive program for students with autism spectrum disorders using evidence-based practices. *Education & Training in Developmental Disabilities, 42*(4), 398-409.

National Autism Center. (2009). *Findings and conclusions of the national standards project.* Obtained electronically on November 28, 2010 at http://www.nationalautismcenter.org/pdf/NAC%20Findings%20&%20Conclusions.pdf.

Office of Revisor Statutes, State of Minnesota. (2007). *Minnesota statutes 2007: Chapter 120B: Curriculum And Assessment.* Retrieved October 3, 2008, from https://www.revisor.leg.state.mn.us/bin/getpub.php?pubtype=STAT_CHAP&year=2007&section=120B

Oetter, P., Richter, E. W., & Frick, S. M. (1993). *M.O.R.E.: Integrating the mouth with sensory and postural functions* (First Complete Edition ed.). Hugo, MN: PDP Press, Inc.

Prizant, B. M., Wetherby, A. M., Rubin, E., Laurent, A. C., & Rydell, P. J. (2006). *The SCERTS model: A comprehensive educational approach for children with autism spectrum disorders (Volume 1: Assessment).* Baltimore, MD: Paul H. Brookes Publishing Co.

Quill, K. (Ed.). (1995). *Teaching children with autism: Strategies to enhance communication and socialization.* Albany, NY: Delmar.

Riccomini, P. J., Zhang, D., & Katsiyannis, A. (2005). Promising school-based interventions for reducing aggressive behavior and student dropout. *The Journal of at-Risk Issues, 11*(2), 11-16.

Spencer, E. D; DuPont, R. L.; & DuPont, C. M. (2003). *The anxiety cure for kids.* Hoboken, NJ: Paul Wiley and Sons, Inc.

Sergeant, J. A., Geurts, H., & Oosterlaan, J. (2002). How specific is a deficit of executive functioning for attention-deficit/hyperactivity disorder? *Behavioural Brain Research. Special Issue: Neurobehavioural Mechanisms in ADHD, 130*(1-2), 3-28.

Simonds, J., Kieras, J. E., Rueda, M. R., & Rothbart, M. K. (2007). Effortful control, executive attention, and emotional regulation in 7-10-year-old children. *Cognitive Development, 22*(4), 474-488.

Simpson, R. L. (2005). Evidence-based practices and students with autism spectrum disorders. *Focus on Autism and Other Developmental Disabilities, 20*(3), 140.

Simpson, R. L., & Myles, B. S. (1998). Aggression among children and youth who have Asperger's syndrome: A different population requiring different strategies. *Preventing School Failure, 42*(4), 149-153.

Sofronoff, K., Attwood, T., & Hinton, S. (2005). A randomized controlled trial of a CBT intervention for anxiety in children with Asperger syndrome. *The Journal of Child Psychology and Psychiatry and Allied Disciplines, 46*(11), 1152-1160.

Sofronoff, K., Attwood, T., Hinton, S., & Levin, I. (2007). A randomized controlled trial of a cognitive behavioural intervention for anger management in children diagnosed with Asperger syndrome. *Journal of Autism and Developmental Disorders, 37*(7), 1203-1214.

Swaggart, B. L. (1998). Implementing a cognitive behavior management program. *Intervention in School and Clinic, 33*(4), 235-238.

Winner, M. G. (2000) *Inside Out: What Makes A Person with Social Cognitive Deficits Tick?* San Jose, CA: Social Thinking Publishing.

Winner, M. G. (2007). *Thinking About YOU Thinking About ME.* San Jose, CA: Social Thinking Publishing.

Winner, M. G. (2005). *Think Social!* San Jose, CA: Social Thinking Publishing.

Williams, M. S., & Shellenberger, S. (1994). *"How does your engine run?" A leader's guide to the alert program for self-regulation.* Albuquerque, NM: TherapyWorks, Inc.

Zero to Three. (1994). *Diagnostic classification of mental health and developmental disorders of infancy and early childhood.* Arlington, VA.

Acknowledgments

I want to thank my family first and foremost. Mom and Dad, thank you for all the guidance and support throughout the years. You have taught me the value of education and demonstrated the importance of going the extra mile and pushing yourself harder. My husband David — I am so grateful to have you in my life as my best friend. Thanks for all the extra things you have done to make this work. My son Daniel, you brighten each day with your smiles and laughter.

I would not have started this project if it were not for the persuasion of Donna Brittain and Susan Friest and their insistence that I had a good idea that needed to be shared. And thank you to all the other amazing staff at Intermediate School District 917 in Dakota County, Minnesota, who adopted The Zones into their classrooms/practices and shared with me their experiences and ideas as I was developing the curriculum: Sherry Peterson, Cathy Mattice, Estelle Garcia, Carrie Koenigsberger, Amy Griff, Joe Faulkner, Berdetta Lang, Crystal DeGraw, Andrea Welveart, Sara Orthaus, and Sara Tuvey. Also, thanks to those at District 196: Rosemount, Apple Valley, Eagan in Minnesota, especially Martha Foster, Jill Kuzma, Jackie Young, and the Autism Resource Specialists, for their input into and implementation of The Zones. A big thanks to the amazing Kari Dunn Buron and Cassandra Erkens for their advice and guidance in writing and developing the curriculum. Thank you to Michelle Garcia Winner for your inspiration as well as for taking on my project and valuable advice. Many thanks to Ann Pendley and Sandy Horwich for all the edits and insights, and Elizabeth Blacker for the amazing transformation in graphic design. Many thanks to Elizabeth Sautter, Hillary Kissack, Lauren Delucci, Erica Bland, Liz Lang, Anthony Savala and those at Communication Works in Oakland, California, for taking a chance on me and helping me to launch The Zones in California. I truly appreciate your support, ideas, feedback, and enthusiasm. Last, thank you to all the students and families I have worked with over the years. Letting me into your lives inspired me to create The Zones with the hope of helping you find a lifetime of success and happiness.

Social Thinking® books, curriculum, thinksheets, and related products developed by Michelle Garcia Winner and Social Thinking Publishing

Core Books About the Social Thinking Model and Curriculum

Thinking About YOU Thinking About ME, 2nd Edition

Think Social! A Social Thinking Curriculum for School-Age Students

Inside Out: What Makes a Person with Social Cognitive Deficits Tick?

Social Behavior Mapping: Connecting Behavior, Emotions and Consequences Across the Day (also available in Spanish)

Why Teach Social Thinking?

For Early Learners

The Incredible Flexible You™: A Social Thinking Curriculum for the Preschool and Early Elementary Years — co-authored by Ryan Hendrix, Kari Zweber Palmer, and Nancy Tarshis

We Can Make It Better! A Strategy to Motivate and Engage Young Learners in Social Problem-Solving Through Flexible Stories — by Elizabeth M. Delsandro

For School-Age Children

You Are a Social Detective! — co-authored by Pamela Crooke (also available in French and Spanish)

Superflex... A Superhero Social Thinking Curriculum — co-authored by Stephanie Madrigal

Superflex Takes on Rock Brain and the Team of Unthinkables — by Stephanie Madrigal

Superflex Takes on Glassman and the Team of Unthinkables — co-authored by Stephanie Madrigal

Superflex Takes on Brain Eater and the Team of Unthinkables — co-authored by Stephanie Madrigal

Superflex Takes on One-Sided Sid, Un-Wonderer, and the Team of Unthinkables — co-authored by Stephanie Madrigal

Social Town Citizens Discover 82 New Unthinkables for Superflex to Outsmart! — co-edited by Stephanie Madrigal

Superflex Superdecks: Card Games to Promote Superflexible Social Thinking

Thinkables & Unthinkables Double Deck

Movie Time Social Learning — by Anna Vagin

Thinksheets for Teaching Social Thinking and Related Skills

Should I or Shouldn't I™? A Game to Encourage Social Thinking and Social Problem Solving, elementary school edition — by Dominique Baudry

Sticker Strategies: Practical Strategies to Encourage Social Thinking and Organization, 2nd Edition

Whole Body Listening Larry at Home! — by Kristen Wilson and Elizabeth Sautter

Whole Body Listening Larry at School! — by Elizabeth Sautter and Kristen Wilson

I Get It! Building Social Thinking and Reading Comprehension Through Book Chats — by Audra Jensen

The Zones of Regulation®: A Curriculum Designed to Foster Self-Regulation and Emotional Control — by Leah M. Kuypers

What is a Thought? (A Thought is a Lot!) — by Jack Pransky and Amy Kahofer